Matching pairs

Draw a line to connect the matching pairs. Then, can you find and circle the odd one out?

1
2
3
4
5
6
7
8
9
10
11

Answer on page 263

Corny joke

What has a bottom at its top?

A leg!

Fun puzzler

My grandpa used to have a group of hens and cows on his farm, that together had a total of 110 heads and feet. How many are there of each type of animal if the hens were twice as many as the cows?

Answer on page 263

4

Connect the dots

Connect the dots to see the picture.

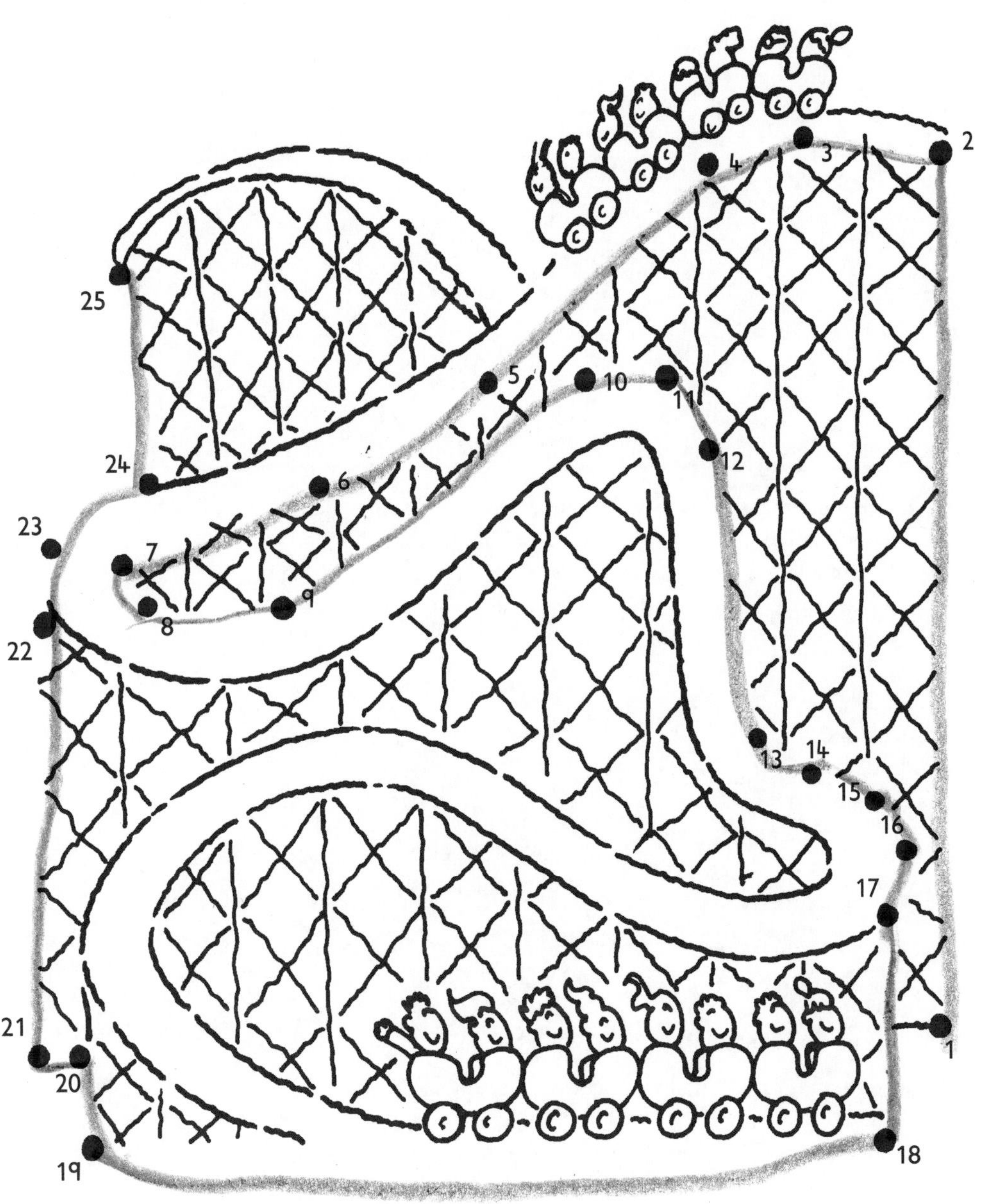

The picture is of ___________

Where can you find it? _______________

Answer on page 263

Monkey maze

The monkey is very hungry. Can you help him find the path with most bananas?

Answer on page 263

Memory game

Look at the pictures on this page carefully for one minute. Then close the book and see how many items you can remember. You can try this with your friends and have a competition.

Odd one out

One of these does not go with the others. Which one is it?

The odd one out is ___________

Answer on page 263

Number joke

Why did the golfer wear an extra pair of trousers?

In case he got a hole in one!

9

Squirrels high and low

Color the highest number in red and the lowest in green. Then put the numbers in order, with the lowest number first.

The numbers in order are: ______________________________

____

Answer on page 263

Vacation horror

You are going to the coast, but the train is crowded and you get bumped and jostled all the way. What could you suffer from riding on such overcrowded TRAINS? (Try rearranging the letters).

I think that you could suffer from ___________

Answer on page 263

Joke time

If 20 dogs run after one dog, what time is it?

Twenty after one!

Fair crossword

The clues and pictures will help you to fill in the grid.

Across
1. Sweet and cold

Down
1. Goes with fish

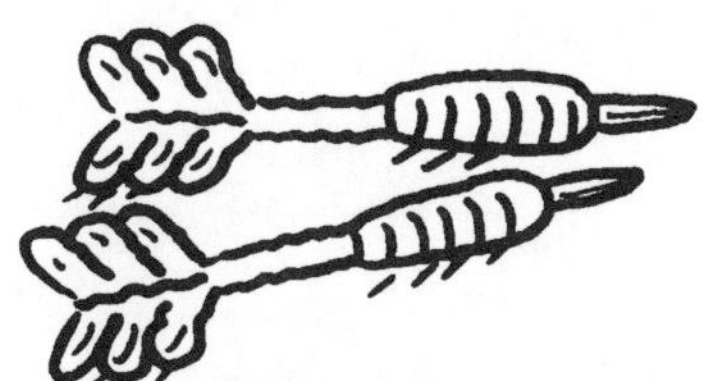

Down
3. Throw to score

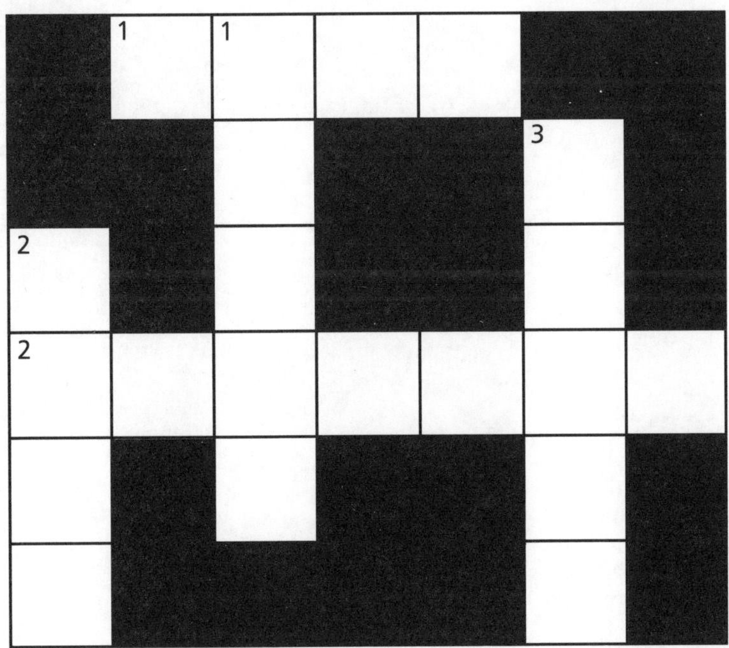

Across
2. Noisy snack

Down
2. You hope the shop is ....

Answer on page 263

Broken words

The names of six animals are broken. Draw lines to join them.

The animals are ______________, ______________, ____________,

______________, ______________ and ______________

Answer on page 263

No joke!

Can you work out the joke?
EREHW SEOD GNIK GNOK PEELS?

EREHWYNA EH STNAW OT!

Answer on page 263

Spot the differences

These monkeys are twins. If you look carefully you will find 10 differences. Can you find and circle them?

Now you can color the pictures of the monkeys.

Answer on page 264

Pharaoh's curse

The professor has opened the mummy's tomb and found that he is going to be very unlucky, unless he can crack the code and remove the Pharaoh's curse. Can you help him?

The message reads:

Answer on page 264

Corny joke

Which years do kangaroos like best?

Kangaroos like LEAP years best.

Matching pairs

Draw a line to connect the flags with their matching sand castles. Then you can color the picture.

Answer on page 264

19

Fun quiz

What is a baby elephant called? Please circle the correct answer.

a. a foal

b. a rhino

c. a calf

Answer on page 264

20

Connect the dots

Connect the dots to see the picture. Then color it in.

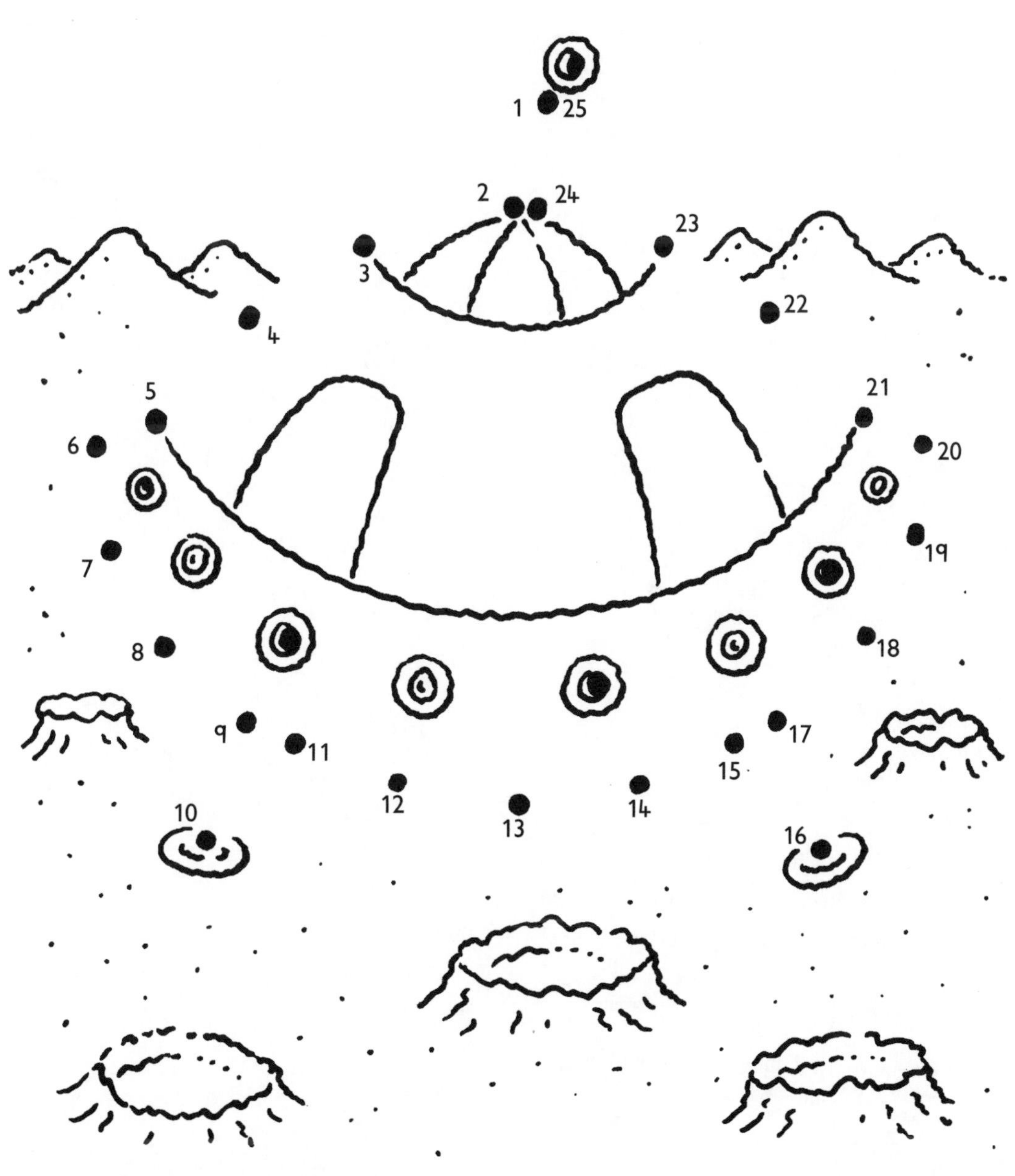

The picture is of a ____________________

Answer on page 264

Amazing

Only the path to number 3 is open. Can you help the mailman find the right path to deliver the postcards to house number 3?

The mailman must take path _____

Answer on page 264

Fido

What type of dog does Dracula keep as a pet?

A BLOODhound

Memory game

Look at the picture for one minute. Then close the book and say which items you can remember.

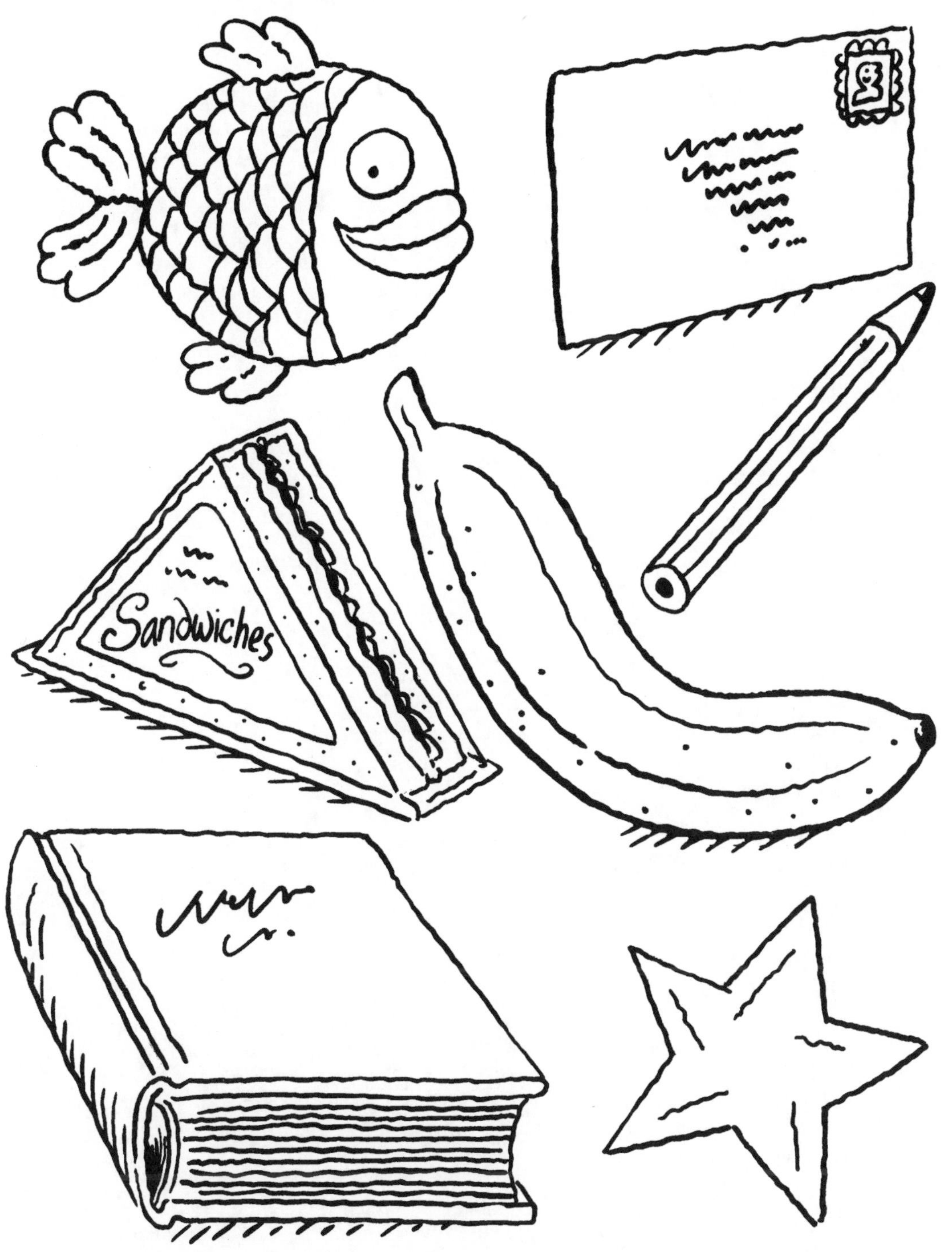

Odd one out

One of these does not go with the others. Which one is it?

The odd one out is the ______________

Answer on page 264

Color fun

Work out the problems on each door of the castle and color the door and the matching window using the same color.

Answer on page 264

Spot the differences

The two pictures of Leo the lion are different in 10 ways. Can you find and circle the differences?

Answer on page 265

Space word wheel

Write the first letter of each picture in the boxes, to spell out a new word about outer space.

The new space word is ____________________

Answer on page 265

Crossword

The numbers show where each word goes in the grid. The clues are in the pictures. Can you guess the words and complete the grid?

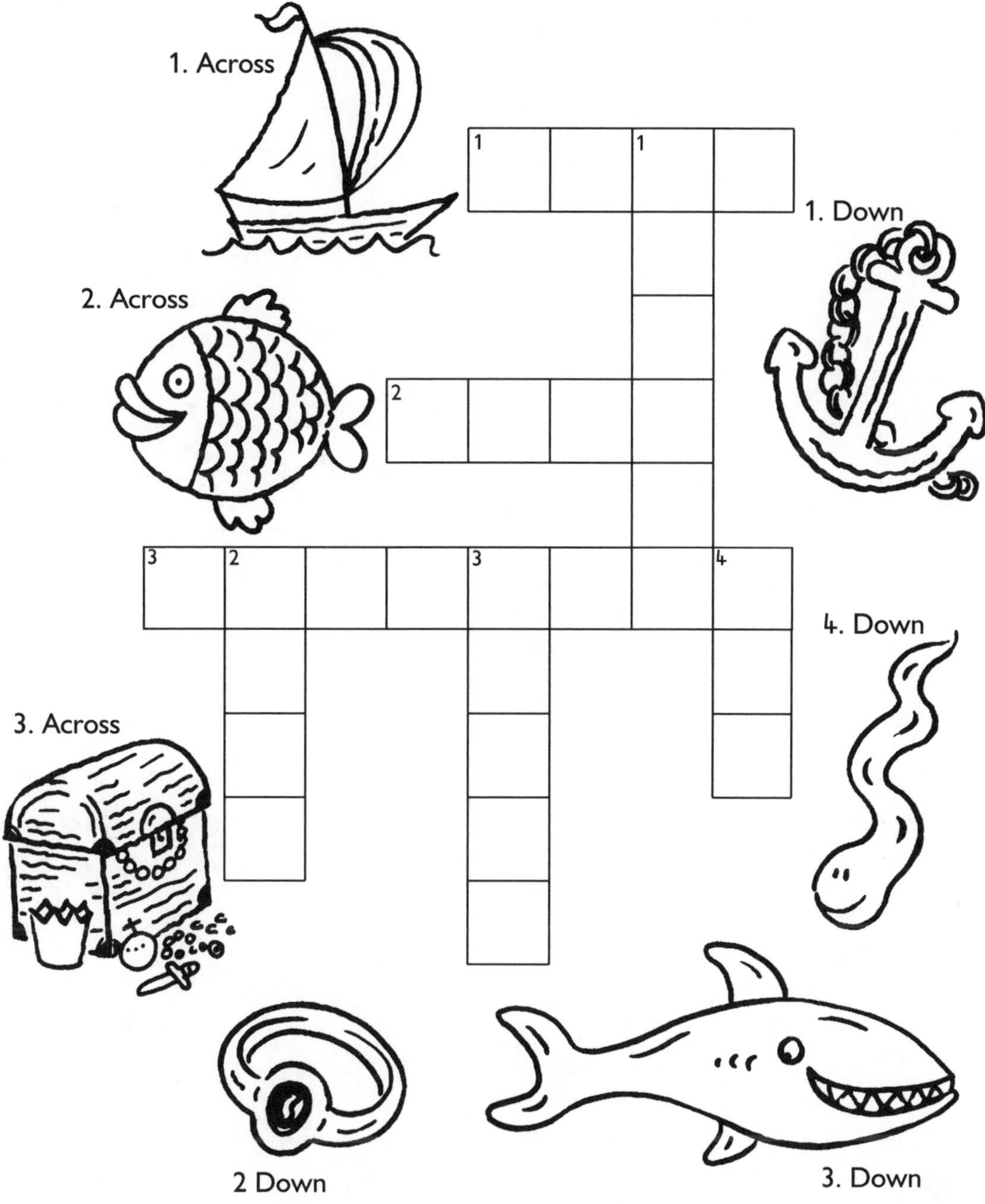

Answer on page 265

I wonder

Where could I have got that puncture?

Perhaps it was the fork in the road!

Speedy?

Look at the pairs. Find which is the quicker way to travel of the two and tick (✓) the correct box.

Answer on page 265

Fun quiz

Tick (✓) the animals which live along the river bank.

Answer on page 265

Connect the dots

Connect the dots to see the picture.

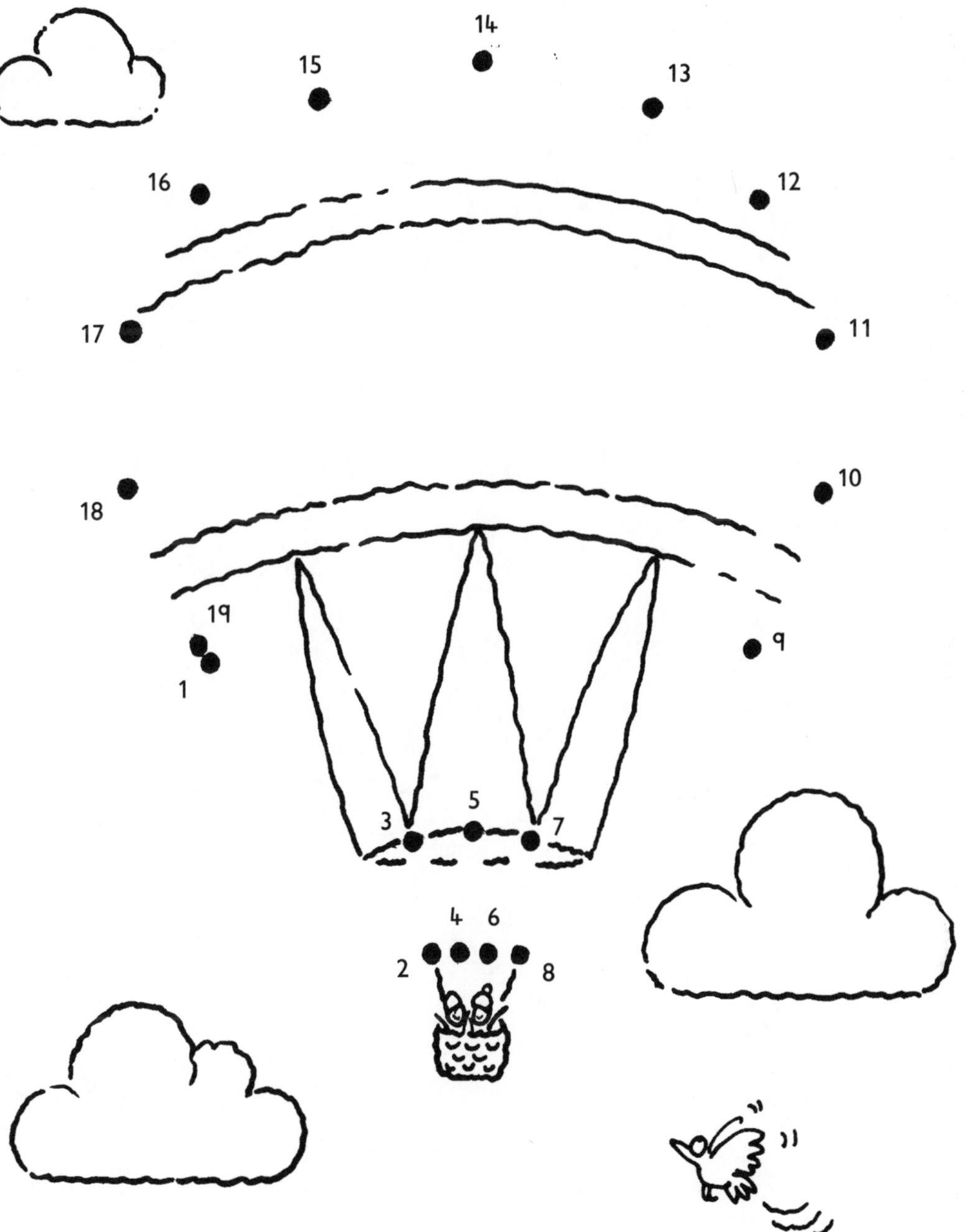

The picture shows a ____________

Answer on page 265

Picture this

The artist knows who the spy is. Follow the arrowed line to find which picture shows the spy.

The spy is B

Answer on page 265

Memory game

Study the picture for one minute. Then close the book and say which items you can remember.

Funny?

What has 50 legs and yet cannot walk?

Half a centipede!

Odd one out

One of these birds does not go with the others. Can you find which one it is and why?

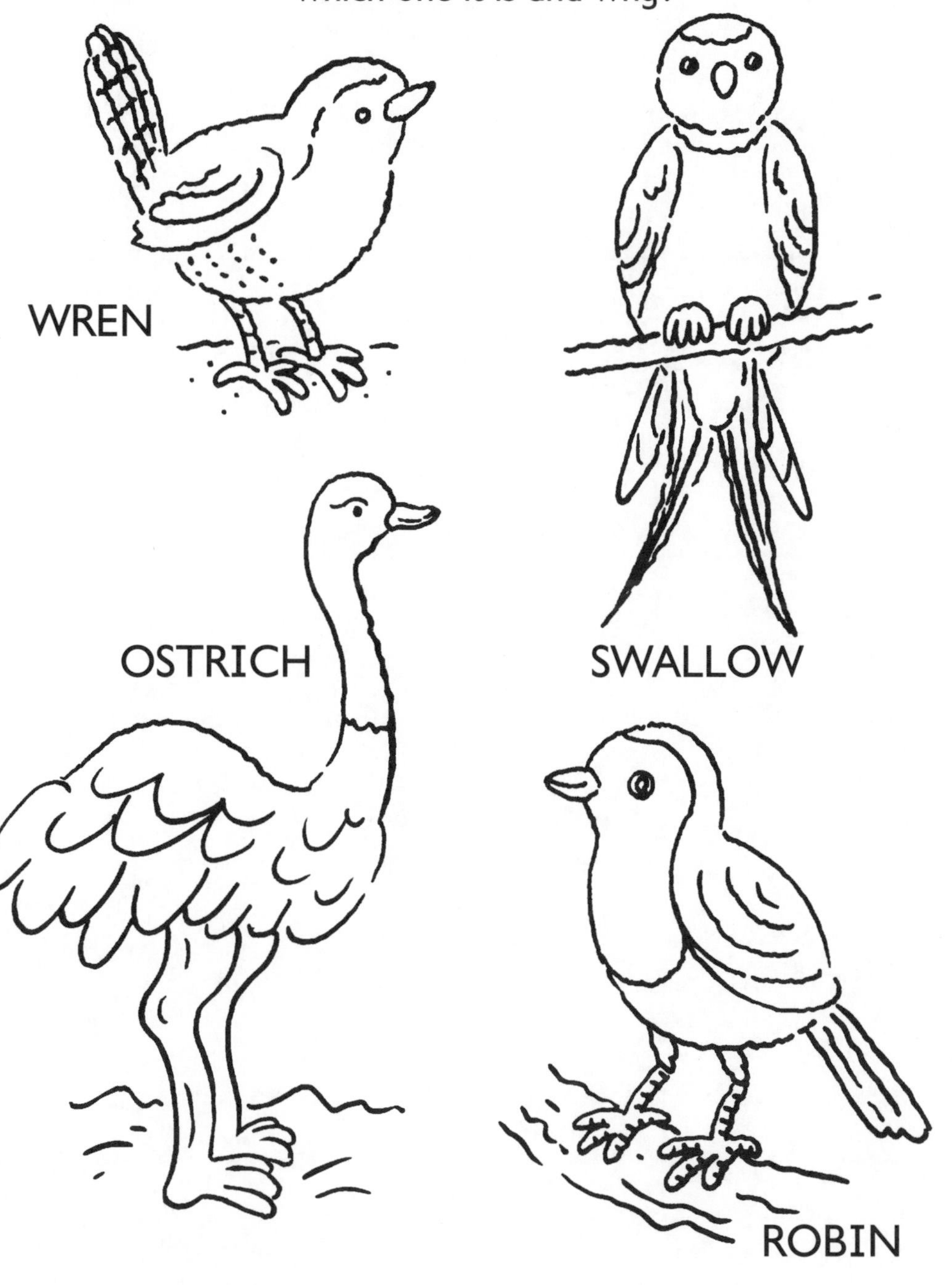

The odd bird out is the ____________ because ____________

____

Answer on page 265

Complete picture

Use the grid to help you to complete this picture.

Complete picture

Spot the differences

The two pictures of this Crocodile are different in 10 ways. Can you find and circle the differences?

Answer on page 266

39

Help!

What is this ancient Egyptian saying? Use the code wheel to find out.

Answer on page 266

(40)

Crossword

All the words in this crossword are about cars, and the pictures are clues.

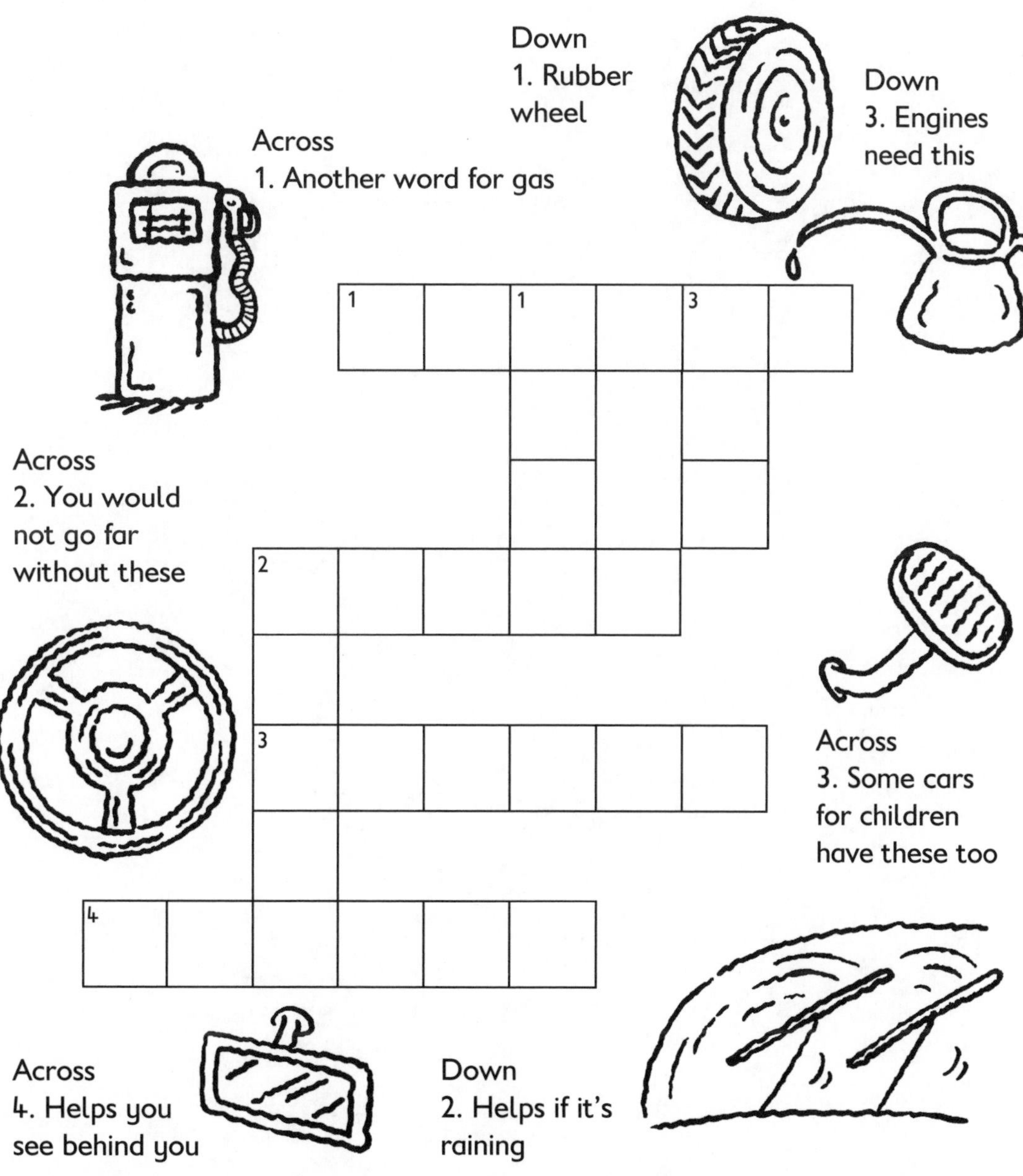

Across
1. Another word for gas
2. You would not go far without these
3. Some cars for children have these too
4. Helps you see behind you

Down
1. Rubber wheel
2. Helps if it's raining
3. Engines need this

Can you think of anything else to do with cars (like horns)?

Answer on page 266

Jelly

What happened after the jellyfish got married?

They had jelly babies.

Matching pairs

Draw lines to join the matching pairs of trains. Then color in all the trains that match and leave the odd one out.

Which is the odd one out?

The odd one out is ___________

Answer on page 266

Fun quiz

Do you know to which continent Italy belongs?
Africa, Antarctica, Asia, Australia, Europe, N. America or S. America?

Italy belongs to ___________________

Can you color the Italian flag in the picture? Can you think of any Italian foods? ______________________________________

Answer on page 266

Connect the dots

Connect the dots to see the picture.

The picture is ____________

Answer on page 266

Spy maze

Trace the lines from empty circles until you find a letter, then copy this letter into the empty circle. Fill all empty circles in the same way to find the hidden word.

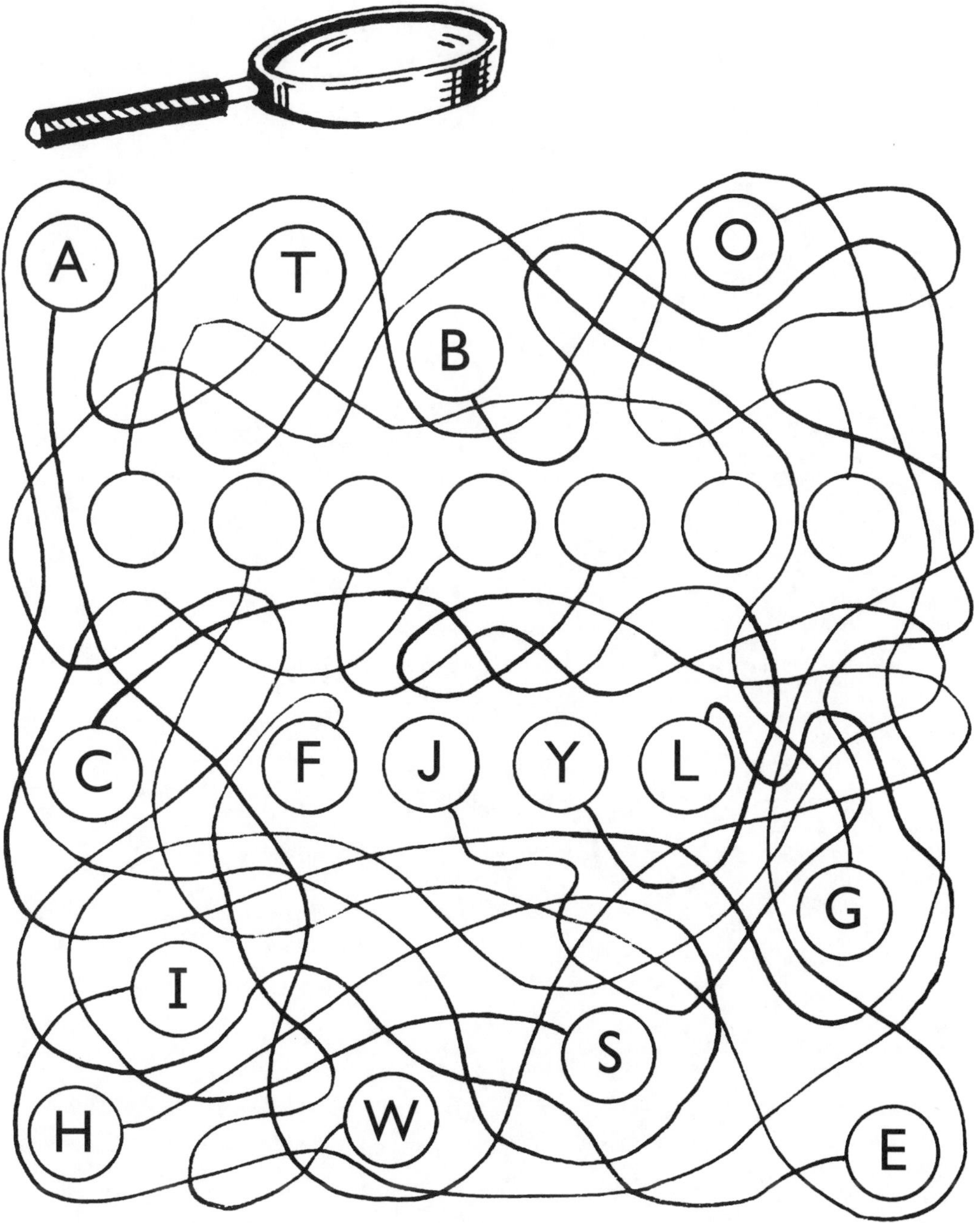

The word that I found is ____________________

Answer on page 266

Memory game

Look at the picture for one minute. Then close the book and say which items you can remember.

Odd one out

One of these does not go with the others. Which one is it?

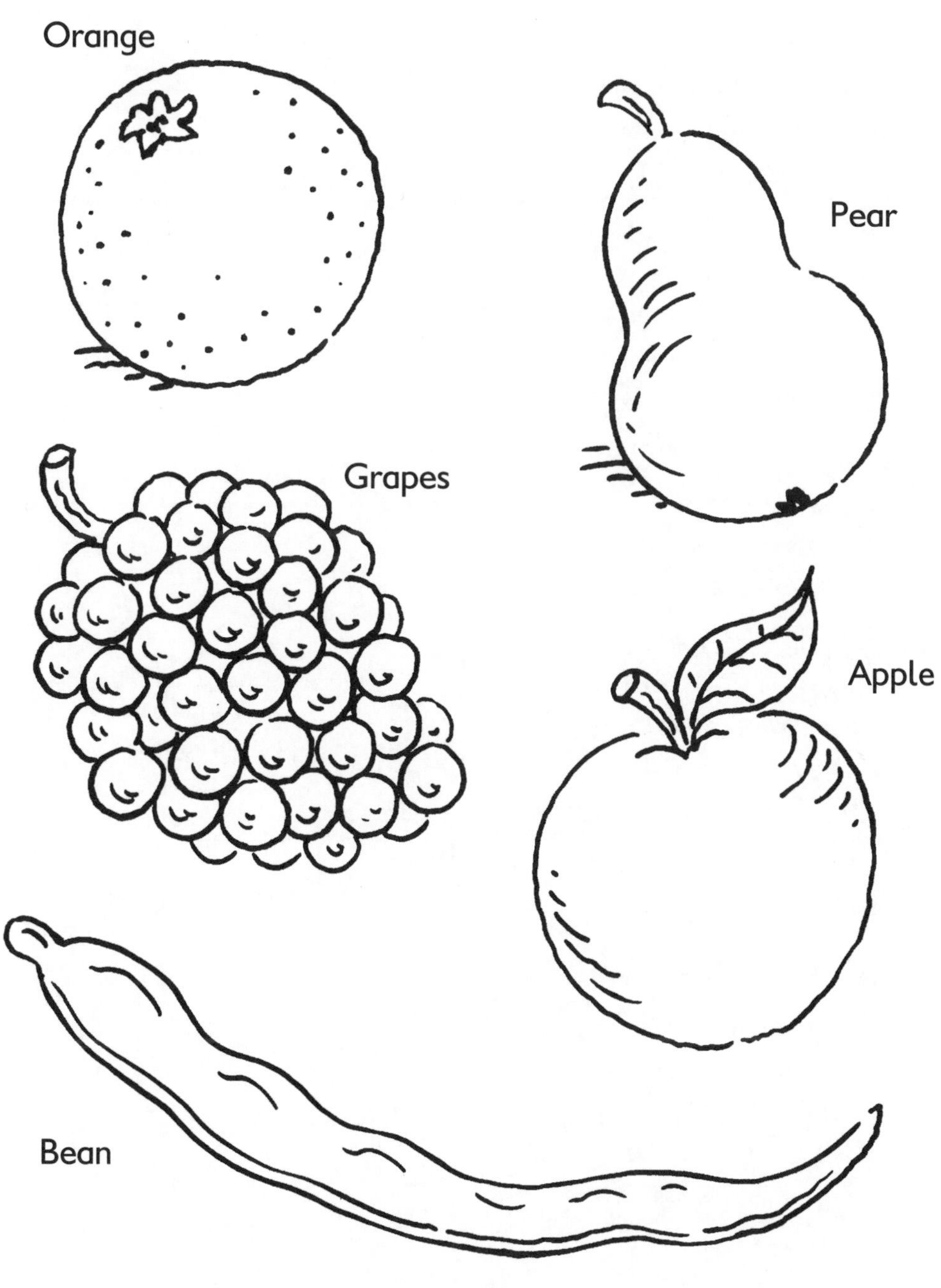

The odd one out is the ____________

Answer on page 266

Complete picture

Use the grid to help you complete this picture.

Spot the differences

There are 10 differences between the two pictures of trucks. Find and circle them. Then, you can color the pictures.

Answer on page 266

Vacation word wheel

Write the first letter of each picture in the boxes, to spell out a new word or phrase about camping.

The words I found are ____________________

Answer on page 266

51

Cross word?

The pictures and written clues will help you to do this crossword. All the answers are moods. Follow the numbers and write the words in the grid.

Down
5. Not mad but...
Across
2. Like an untamed animal
Across
1. Bothered, irritated
Down
4. Like this clue
Down
2. Upset and aggressive
Down
1. Feeling pleased and in good spirits
Down
3. Like a raging fire

Answer on page 266

Cross road

Why did the hedgehog cross the road?

To see her flatmate.

Heavier or lighter?

Look at the pairs and tick (✓) the heavier of the two.

Answer on page 266

Fun quiz

Which is the quickest road to take from Disneyland to the center of Paris? Please tick: (✓)

Answer on page 267

Connect the dots

Connect the dots to see the picture.

6

2 4 1 5 3 20

The picture is ___________

Can you think of another word to use instead? _____________

Answer on page 267

Agent's maze

Which path links the two secret agents?

The path is ________

Answer on page 267

Count the fish

A shark has frightened the little fish away. Can you count the fish that stay, unaware of the shark?

There are _____ fish staying by the shark.

Answer on page 267

Animal crackers

What type of fish do dogs chase?

Catfish!

Odd one out

Can you find the odd one out and say why?

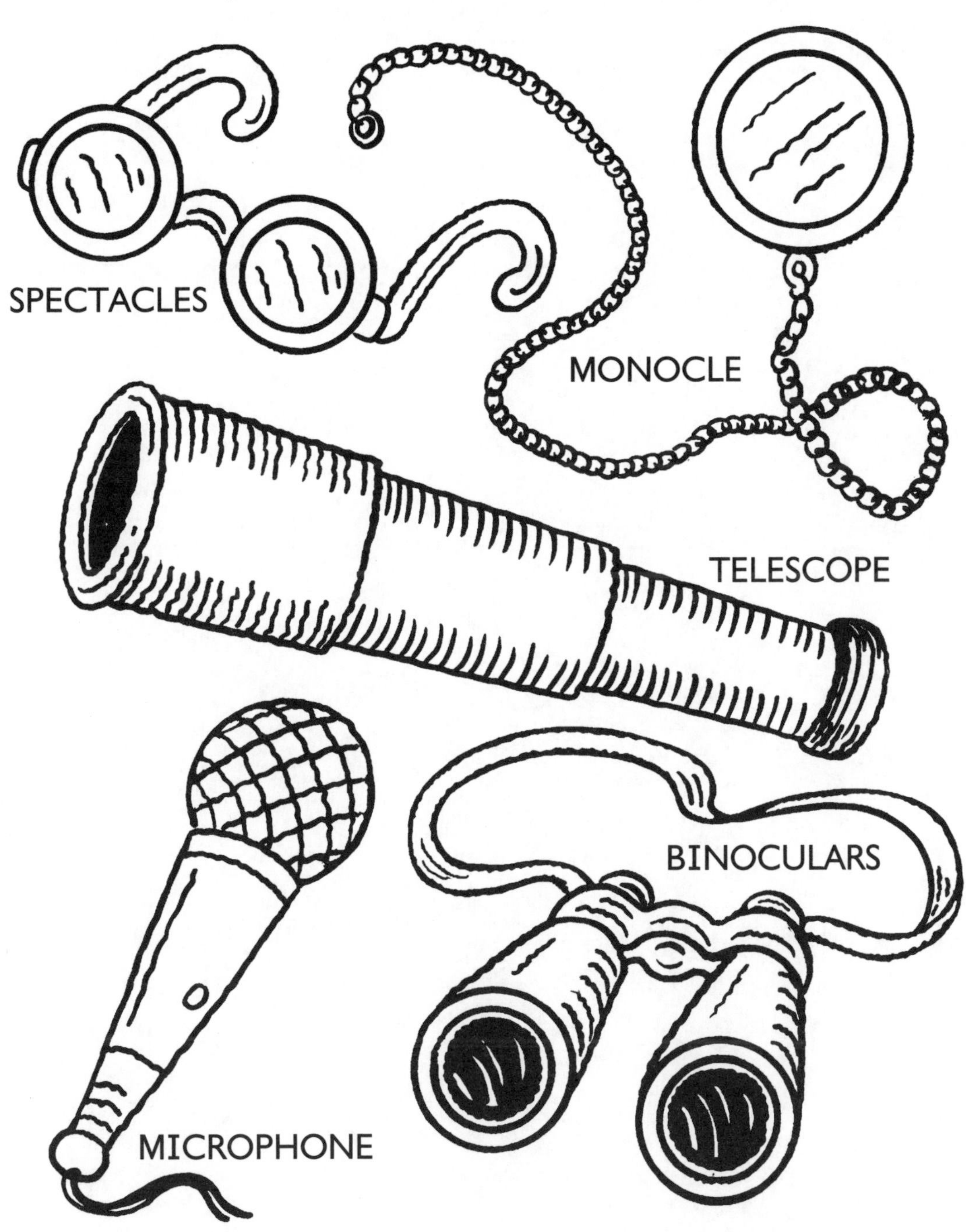

The odd one out is the ______________________________

because ______________________________

Answer on page 267

Fly a kite

Color the additions that make 25.

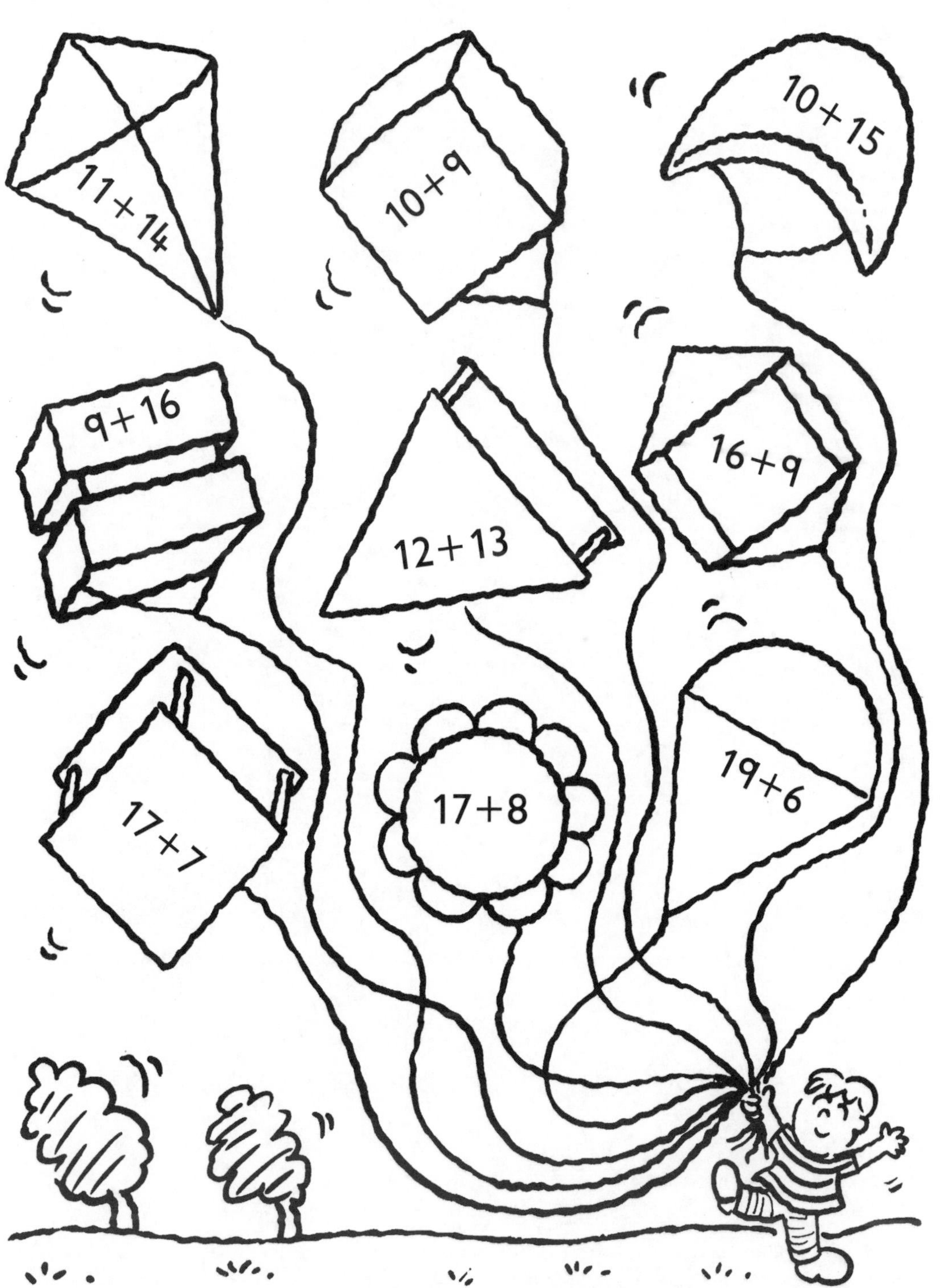

Answer on page 267

Spot the differences

Look at these pictures. They look very similar, yet there are six differences between them. Find them all and put a circle around them.

Answer on page 267

Summertime word wheel

Write the first letter of each picture in the boxes to spell out a new word.

The word I found is ____________________

Answer on page 267

Pirate's dream

Write the name of the pictures in the spaces provided. A hidden word will be discovered in the center column.

Answer on page 268

Tired?

Which bird is always out of breath?

A Puffin.

Fishing

Which fish are caught in which nets?

Answer on page 268

Fun quiz

If two boys eat 2 pizzas in 2 days, how many pizzas will 6 boys eat in 6 days?

Answer on page 268

Connect the dots

Connect the dots to complete the picture.

The picture is of a _______________

Answer on page 268

Amazing

Help the boy to go through the maze and find his vacation resort.

He is going to ____________

Answer on page 268

Count the triangles

How many triangles can you find in this picture?
Color them in.

I found ______ triangles.

Answer on page 268

Odd ones out

Color the odd one out in each row.

Answer on page 268

Half of a scare

Can you complete the picture and color it in?

What's the name?

A famous Egyptian's name is written on the tomb, but nobody knows what it is. The first letter of each picture helps make the name. Can you arrange the letters to read it?

The name is ____________________

Answer on page 268

73

Diamonds are forever

To reach the priceless treasure, you must cross over some treacherous paving stones. Only one from each row is safe. The correct letters will create a secret word. Can you find them?

Answer on page 269

Joke

Why did the spy have two heads?

Have you heard of a double agent?

Spot the differences

Spot the 6 differences on James Bond's car.

Now you can color them.

Answer on page 269

Word wheel – cool spot

Write the first letter of each picture in the boxes to spell out a new phrase.

The word I found is ______________________

Answer on page 269

(77)

Cold and stranded

You are stranded outside a cozy igloo. You must work out the password by filling in the grid. The password will appear on the tinted squares.

1
2
3
Clues:
1 To choose
2 Short form of Crocodile
3 Plants grow from this

To get into the igloo, say the password: ________

Answer on page 269

Lonely Ice

Why did the ice cream cornet cry?

Because its mom had been a waifer too long.

Finishing order

These cars are in a race. The one with the highest number comes first. Draw a line to put the cars in numerical order.

Answer on page 269

Fun quiz

Which is the smallest one of all? Find and circle the right bird.

Answer on page 269

Connect the dots

Draw lines to connect the dots and complete the picture.

The picture is ____________

Name 3 other creatures we find in the sea: ________________

____________________ ____________________

Answer on page 269

Amazing

A robot has landed on a hostile planet and is lost. Can you help it find the way to its spaceship avoiding all the mines?

Answer on page 269

Dinner time

There were 15 bananas in each bunch. How many bananas has the monkey eaten from each bunch?

Answer on page 270

Go South

Why do birds fly south for the winter?

Because they can't walk on water!

Odd bird out

Which is the odd bird out and why do you think so?

The odd bird out is the ____________________

because ____

Answer on page 270

Sunny days

Color the suns that make 20.

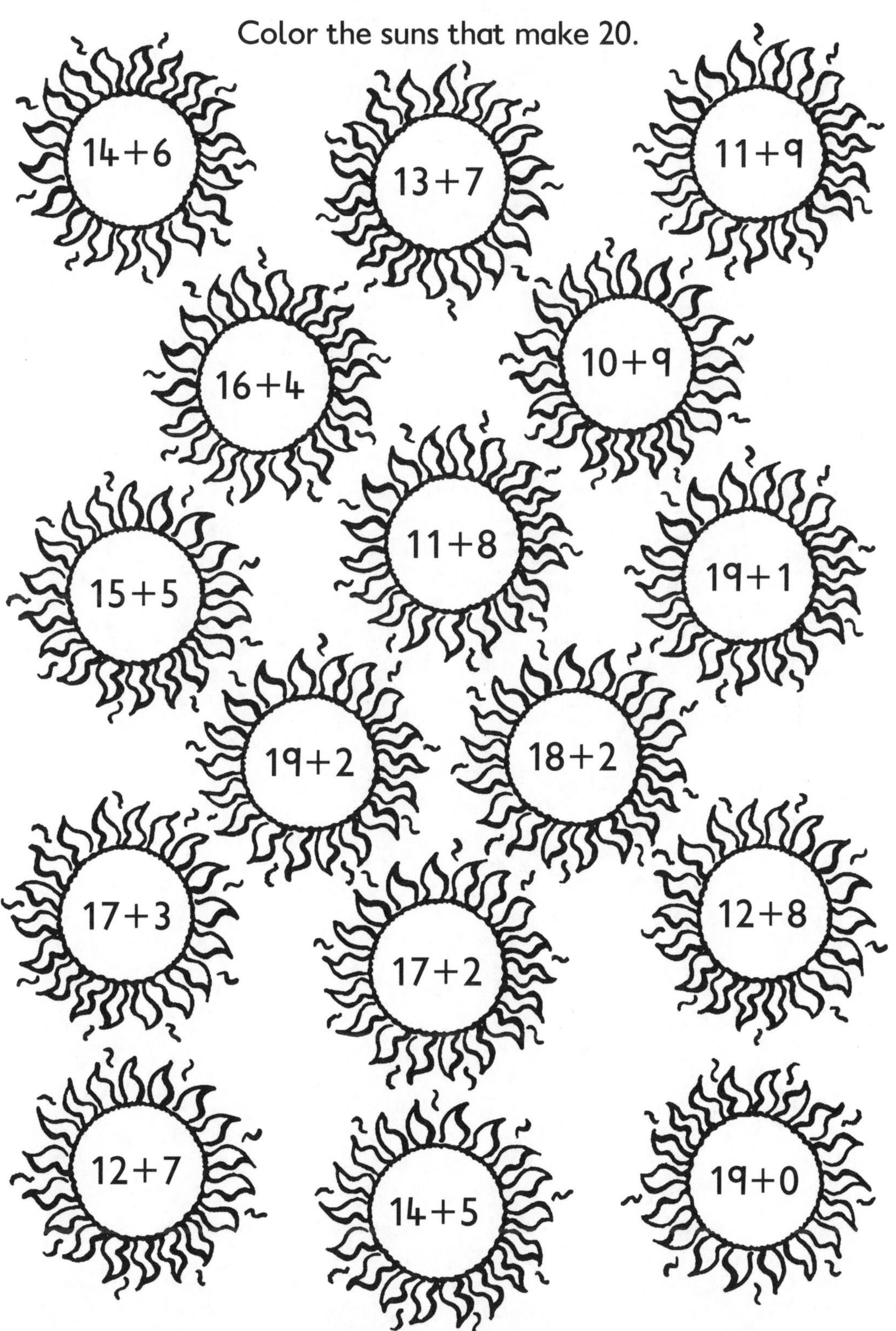

Answer on page 270

In the deep deep forest

The artist has made five errors in this picture. Can you find the errors and circle them?

Answer on page 270

Anagram

Can you unscramble these words?

Answer on page 270

89

Mirror writing

Hold this page in front of a mirror to read the message. What is the message?

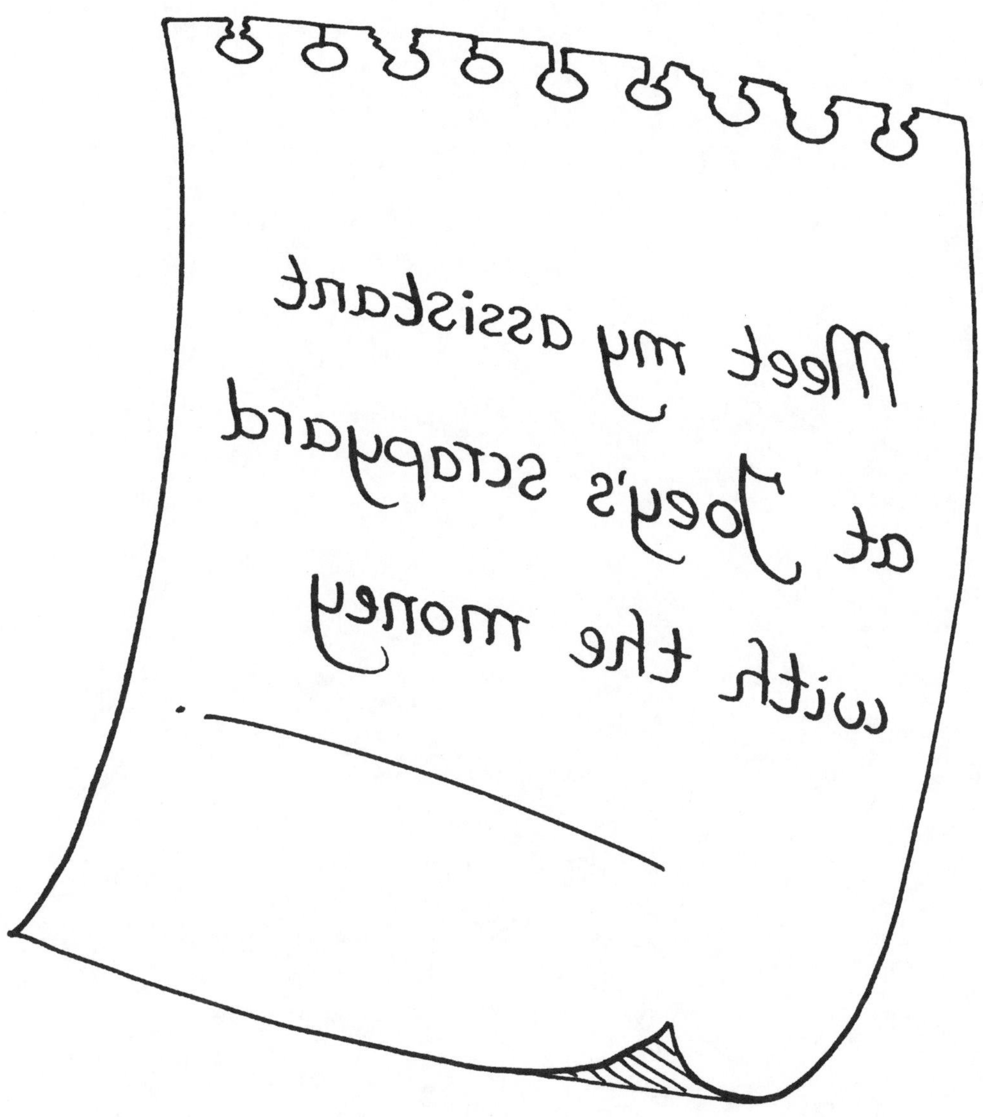

The message is ______________________________

____

Answer on page 270

He's a new boy

What do you do with a spy who is a bit GREEN?

Put him in the sun until he ripens!

Message in a bottle

This message has been washed up on the beach. Use the code wheel to help you decode it.

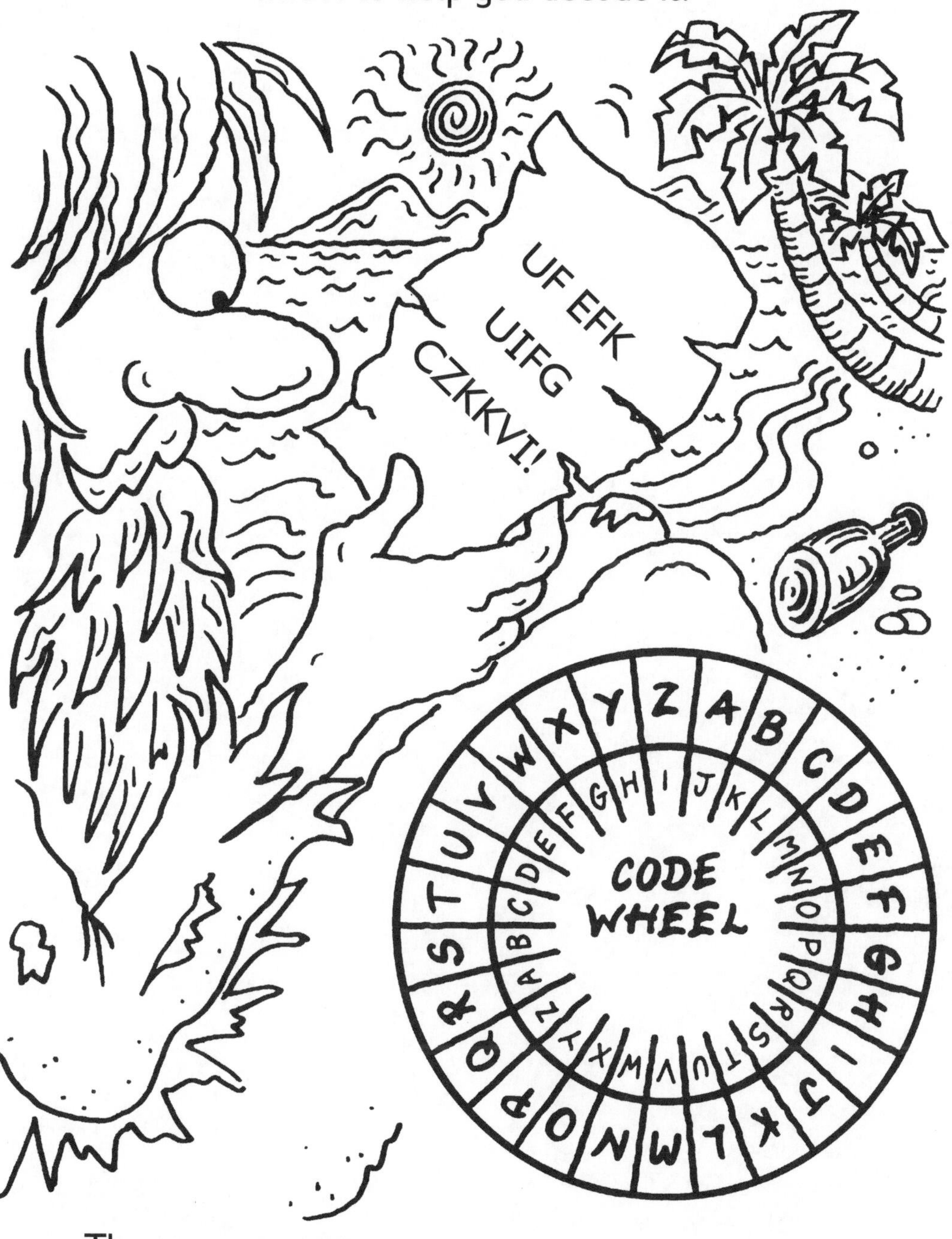

The message says: ____________________

____

____

Answer on page 270

Coast chain words

Write the words into this chain. The clues will help you. The last letter of each word becomes the first one of the next.

Clues
1. Used to make castles
2. Another word for ass
3. Sort of boat
4. Afternoon meals
5. Food for picnics

Answer on page 270

Butterfly beauties

Match pairs of butterflies to add up to 15 spots.

Answer on page 271

Fun puzzle

Can you draw a line to connect the last 5 jig-saw pieces to the right places and complete the puzzle?

1 2 3 4 5

A B C D E

Answer on page 271

Dotty toy

Connect the dots to find the birthday gift.

Amazing

This boy is very hot. Can you help him to find an ice cream?

Answer on page 271

Spot the spots

Count the spots on each fish and write the number on the bubble next to it.

Answer on page 271

Odd one out

One of the words in this list does not belong. Can you find and circle it?

fir
hare
tare
pair
rode
hair
ride
tear
road
fur
pear

Answer on page 271

Fireworks

Add the numbers in each rocket then color 10 in red, 12 in blue and 11 in pink.

Answer on page 271

Coastal Errors

The artist has made 8 mistakes in this seaside picture. Can you find the mistakes and circle them?

Answer on page 272

Word wheel

Write the first letter of each picture to spell out a fun summer activity.

I think that the fun summer activity is ____________

Answer on page 272

(102)

Message in the tomb

A grave robber tries to escape from an Egyptian tomb. He has to pull out either a rectangular, or circular, or triangular stone from the wall. Which is the correct one to open the tomb? Use the snail code on the right to read the message.

1 F	2 Z	3 I	4 E	5 N
8 D	9 A	10 B	11 C	6 G
7 M	12 L	Y	12 K	7 H
6 O	11 P	10 Q	9 R	8 S
5 X	4 W	3 V	2 U	1 T

CZKK FMW

AWPFRXOZ KRA

DFGXW

He should ____________________ to escape.

Answer on page 272

Favorites

Who is Dracula's favorite Jungle-Swinging hero?

Batzan!

Sharing

Can you share the nuts equally between the squirrels in each tree?

Each squirrel will have ______ nuts

Each squirrel will have ______ nuts

Answer on page 272

Fun quiz

Can you find the name of the girl who went RIDING?
(Try rearranging the letters).

Her name is ________.

Answer on page 272

Connect the dots

Draw a line to connect the dots and find what these boys are playing with.

Amazing

Can you help the little boy go through the maze and find out where he will stay during his summer vacation?

During his summer vacation he is going to stay in a

____

Answer on page 272

Amazing

Go through the maze to find out how the girl is going to go on vacation this summer: by air, by road or by ship.

She is going on vacation by ____________

Answer on page 272

How many orders?

The delivery man has mixed up his orders. Can you do the additions and join the orders to the correct houses?

Answer on page 272

110

Odd one out

One of the words in this list does not belong. Which one is it?

SIGHT
HEAL
RAIN
SEE
MAIZE
HART
SEA
EIGHT
MINE
REIN
ATE
SITE
HEART
MAZE
HEEL

The word that does not belong is ________________

Answer on page 272

Color fun

Color in the desert island.

Silly Errors

The artist has made 5 silly errors in this picture. Can you find them?

Answer on page 272

Silly Errors

The artist has made 5 silly errors in this picture. Can you find them?

Word wheel

Write the first letter of each picture to spell out a summer drink.

The summer drink is ________________

Answer on page 272

Pirate's code

Fill in the grids (multiply in the top grid, add in the bottom grid).

X	0	1	2	3	4	5
0			0			
1						
2						
3						

+	0	1	2	3	4	5	6	7
0								
1								
2			4					
3								
4								

Answer on page 273

Rockaby ET

How do you get baby ET to sleep?

Rock-ET

Matching pairs

Draw lines to join the bathing suits that go together.

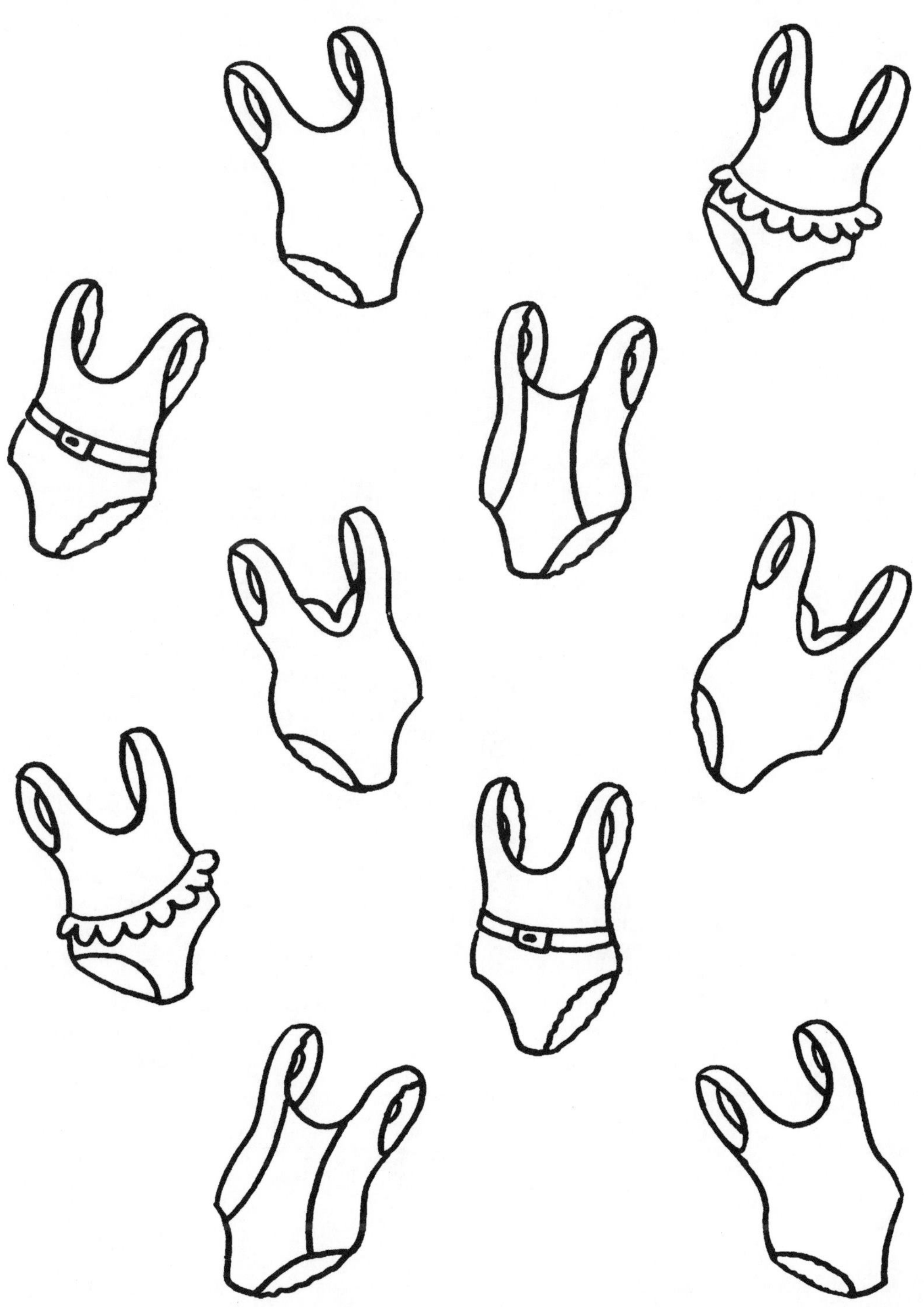

Answer on page 273

Fun quiz

Which is heavier, a ton of feathers or a ton of lead?

I think ___________________

Answer on page 273

Spooky connect the dots

Connect the dots from a to b, then b to c and so on to complete this picture. Then color it in.

Answer on page 273

Anagram

Can you unscramble these words?
Some of them are about spies.

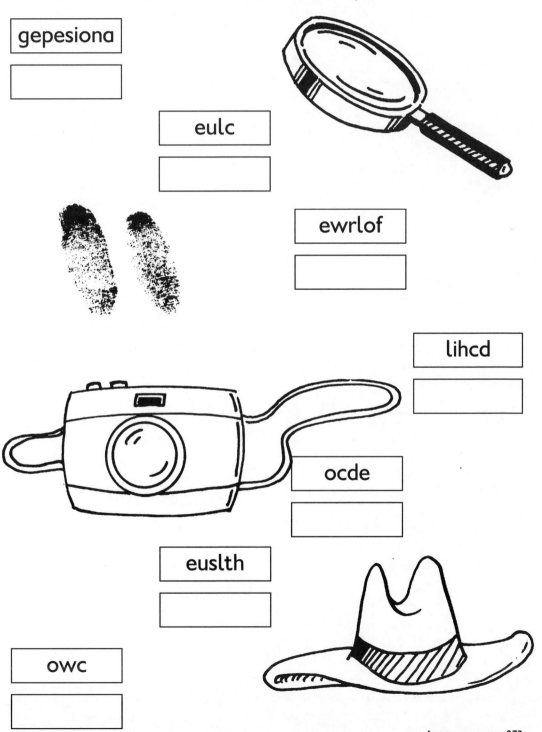

gepesiona

eulc

ewrlof

lihcd

ocde

euslth

owc

Answer on page 273

Invitations

You want to visit your friends and give them an invitation to your party. Can you find in which order you have to visit them so that you reach all of them without going on the same path more than once?

Answer on page 273

Strained?

Why is the spycatcher angry?

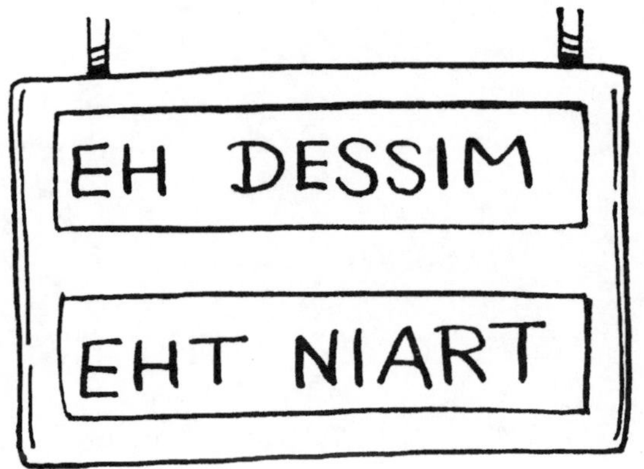

He's angry because ______________________

Answer on page 274

Countdown

Some friends are going on vacation soon. Look at the calendars and find how many days are left until they leave including the days shown.

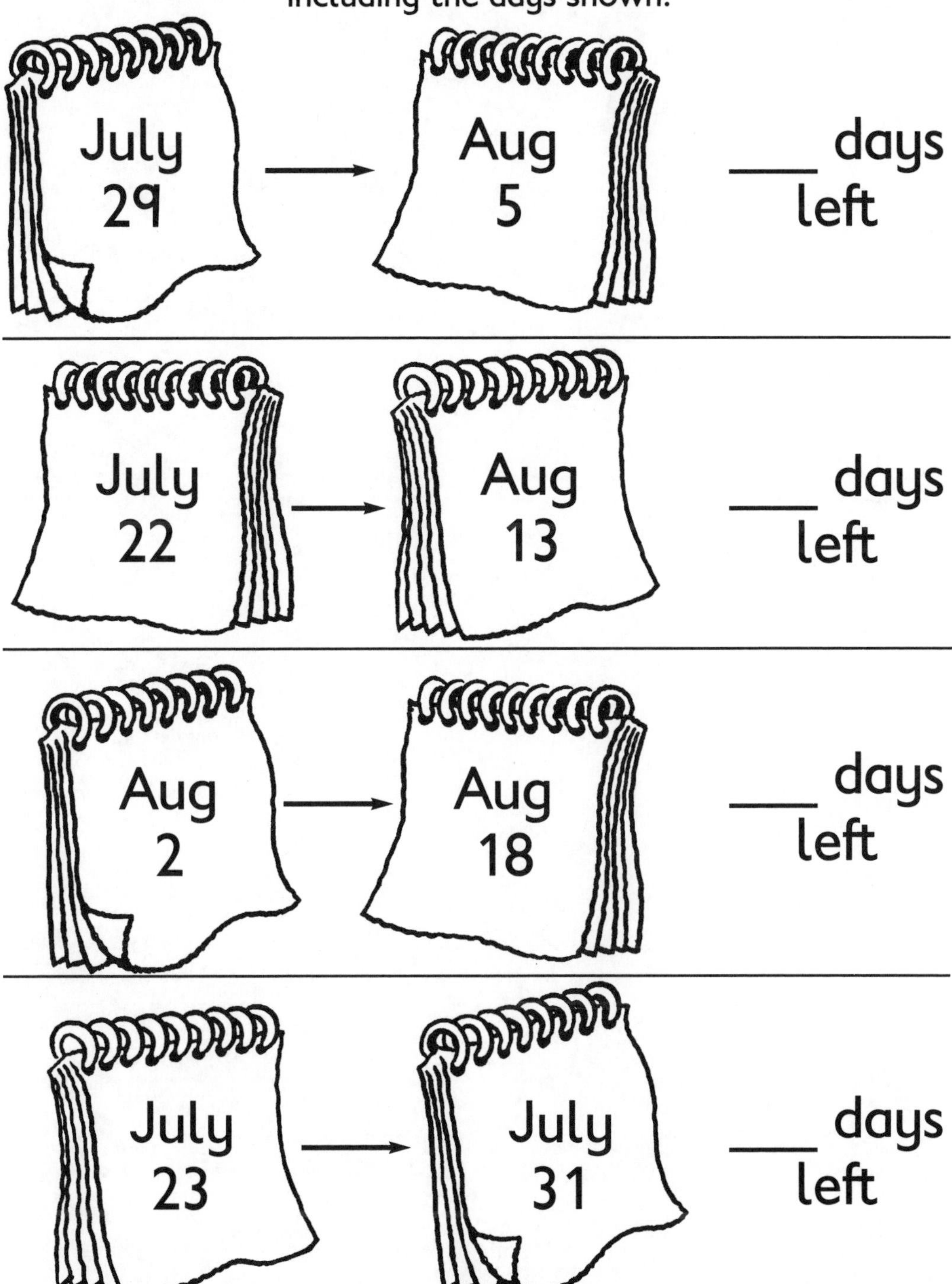

Answer on page 274

Diets

My sister is on a Seafood diet.

As soon as she sees food she eats it.

Odd one out

Which picture is the odd one out? Why?

The odd one out is the ____________________ because

____

Answer on page 274

Color fun

Color in Earth as it is seen from space.

Lost letters

There are eight letters lost in this funfair picture. Can you find and circle them?

The hidden letters are: ____________________

Answer on page 274

Find the city

Jan is going to go to Europe next month. Can you rearrange the letters and find all the European cities she is going to visit?

Answer on page 274

Hidden meaning

A man is looking through the window with binoculars and he sees this sign on a building. What does it mean?

The words are ____________________

Answer on page 274

Hot stuff

What happened to the monster who had too hot a curry?

He spent a week Vindaloo!

Words and pictures

Can you draw a line to join the pictures with their names?

Answer on page 274

Fun quiz

Which is the tallest one of all? Find and circle it.

1 a giraffe

2 a lion

3 a penguin

Answer on page 274

Fun quiz

Which is the tallest one of all? Find and circle it.

1 a giraffe

2 a lion

3 a penguin

Answer on page 224

Connect the dots

Follow the letters and draw lines to complete this picture.

The picture shows a ___________

Answer on page 274

The Marathon maze

Can you find your way through the maze?

Answer on page 275

The Marathon maze

Can you find your way through the maze?

Adding up

Color the buses with the additions that make 20.

36-14

50-30

31-9

42-21

49-29

44-14

27-9

49-30

34-14

40-20

41-21

Answer on page 275

Adding up

Color the buses with the additions that make 20.

Answer on page 275

They nose!

To decode this message, move the alphabet forward by one letter. For example, X=Y so the first word, XNT means YOU.

The note says: ________________________________

____

Answer on page 275

Ghoulish

What is the difference between a man and his ghost?

The man is all grown while his ghost is all groan!

Rhyming pairs

Pairs of words for these pictures rhyme. Can you write the words and connect those which rhyme?

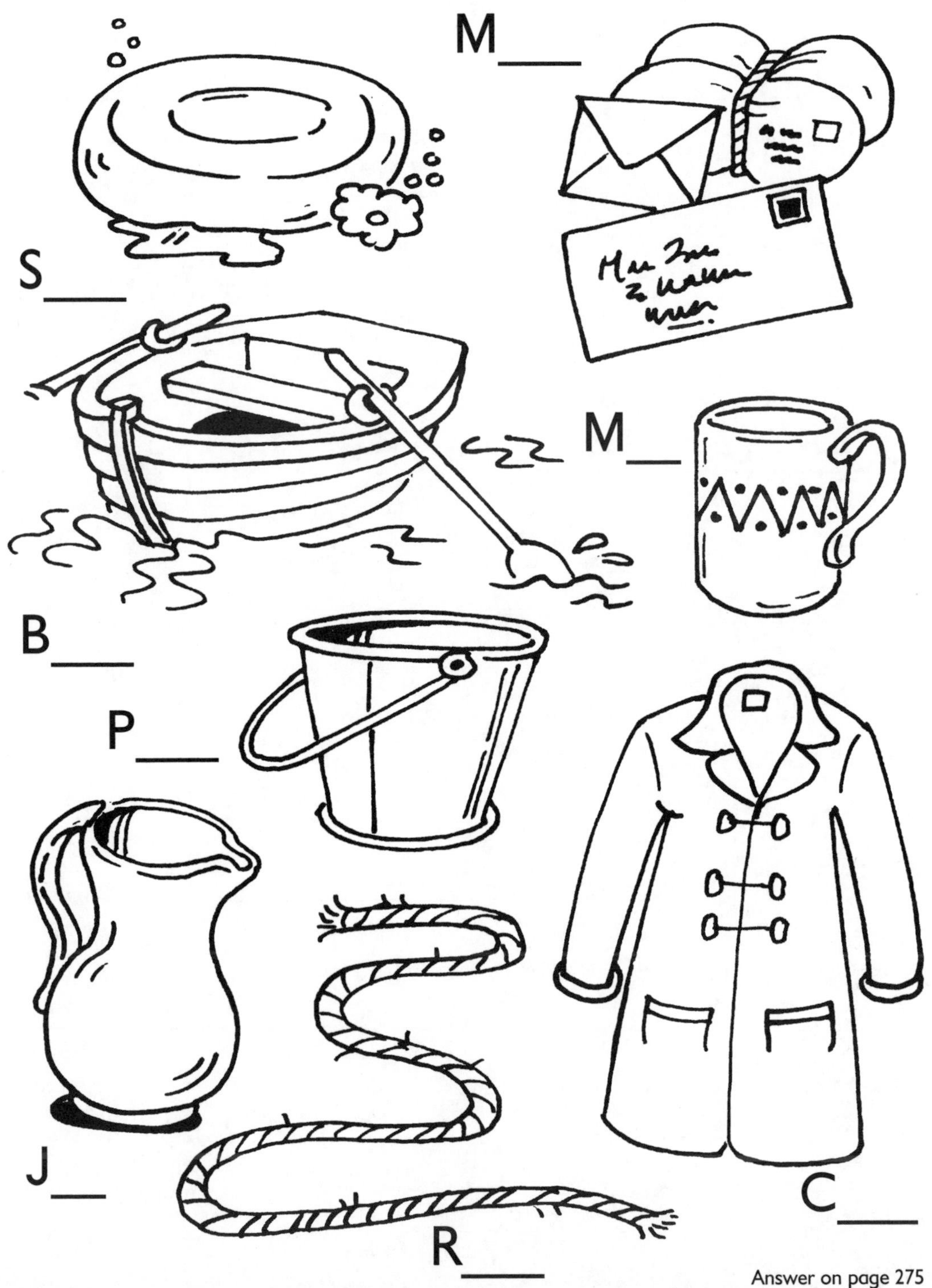

Answer on page 275

Color fun

Color in the cheetah, the fastest creature on the ground.

How many spots are there on the cheetah?

Answer on page 275

Surfing silly errors

The artist has made 5 silly errors. Can you find and circle them?

Use pencils or felt-tips to color the picture.

Answer on page 275

How many words?

The picture shows a nice round hippopotamus. How many new words can you make from the letters in 'hippopotamus'? See if you can make at least five.

I made these words ________, ________, ________,

________, ________, ________, ________,

________, ________, ________, ________, ________

Answer on page 275

Spycatcher

A famous spy receives an urgent message.
Crack the code to read it.

UDZO UNZOUT UCZOUMZE UTZO
ZOZUUR UMZEZEUTZIUNUG. ZI ZAUM
UFZOULULZOUWZEUD.

The message reads ______________________________

____

Answer on page 276

Coach trip

In 1492 which bus crossed the Atlantic?

Christopher ColumBUS

Matching pairs

Draw lines to connect the airplanes that match.

Answer on page 276

Fun puzzle

Rearrange the puzzle pictures to put the snake back together. Then color it in.

Answer on page 276

Sunny connect the dots

Follow the alphabet to complete this picture. Then, color it in.

Fly away maze

Find the control which is linked to the toy airplane.

A B C D

Answer on page 276

Time for lunch

Find how many sausages are left in the pan.

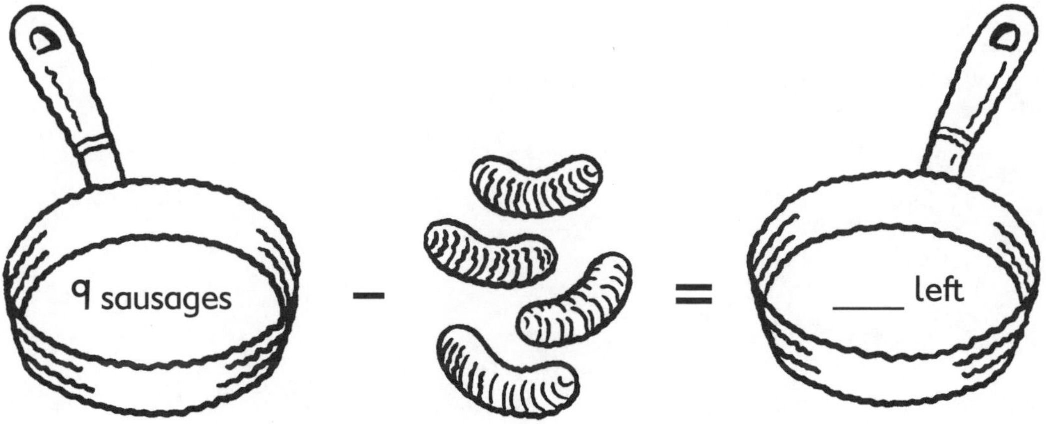

9 sausages − = ____ left

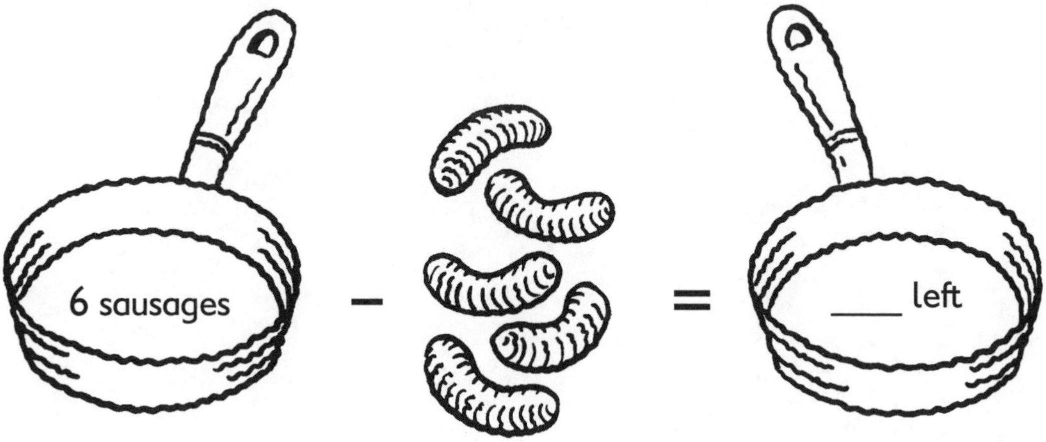

6 sausages − = ____ left

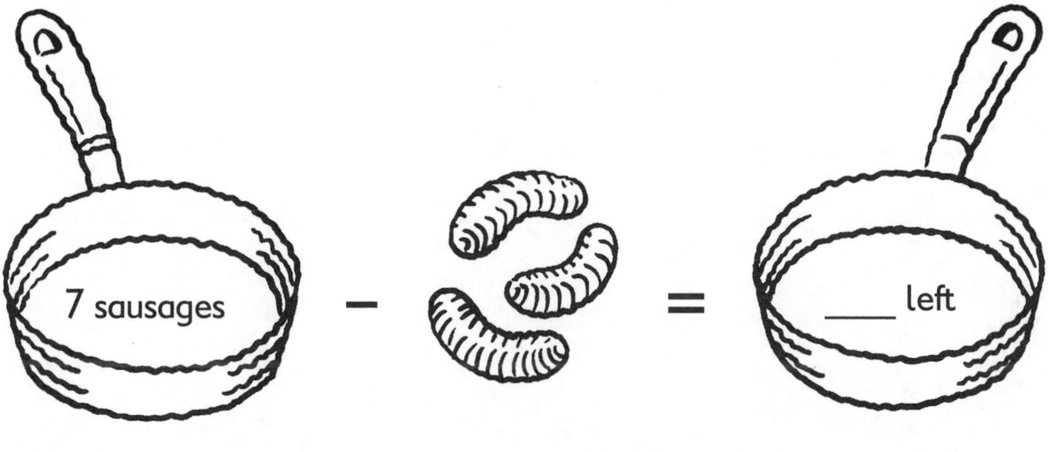

7 sausages − = ____ left

Answer on page 276

Stranded

Which island is like a box?

Cuba!

I Spy unusual buildings

Can you spot these types of building? Color the silhouettes when you see them. Draw a line to connect the names to the correct pictures.

I spotted _____ different types of buildings

Answer on page 276

Fast and slow

Color in red the fastest of each pair.

Answer on page 277

Weather wordsearch

Find 7 weather words and circle them.

S	C	F	R	I	F
U	C	L	O	U	D
N	R	A	I	N	S
W	E	F	R	F	N
H	A	T	E	F	O
F	W	I	N	D	W

Answer on page 277

Find the word

The letters of these words are all mixed up. Can you put them in order and write the correct word on the lines next to them?

NALTEEPO ________________

FRIFGEA ________________

YKMEON ________________

USOME ________________

ROCDCELOI ________________

NEPELHTA ________________

Answer on page 277

Dog's life

Can you find the name of the dog?

Jock

Dusty

Rover

Answer on page 277

Hot water

Who is the most famous Roman plumber?

Julius Geezer.

Matching pairs

Draw lines to connect the balloons that go together. Color them all, apart from the odd one out.

Answer on page 277

Puzzle ice

The mystery ice flavor is spelt using the <u>missing</u> five letters.

The flavor is __________

Answer on page 277

Connect the dots

Connect the dots to find a fierce animal. Then color it in.

Do you know what is the name for a group of such animals?

Answer on page 277

Amazing

Find the way out of the maze and away from the crocodile.

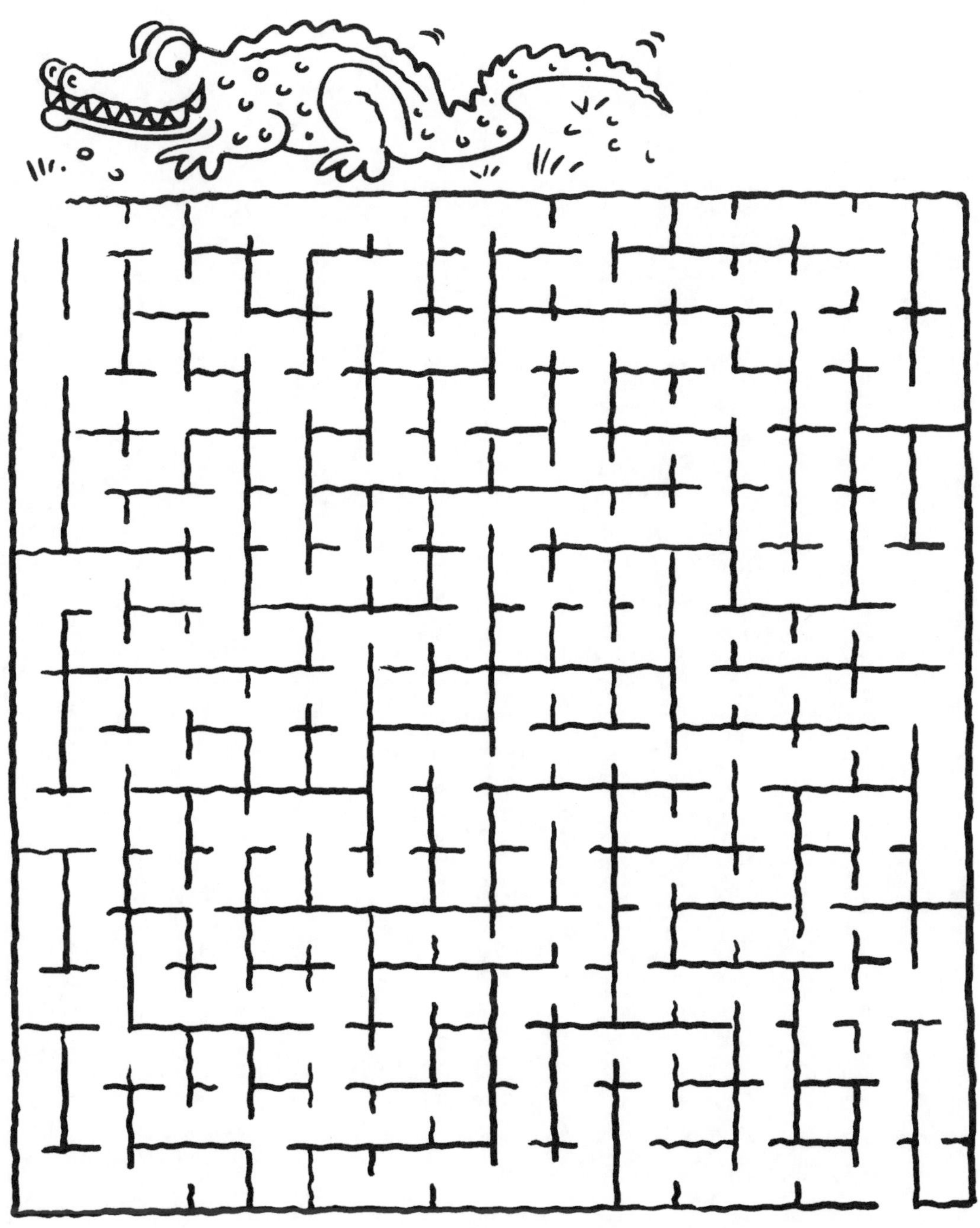

Are crocodiles mammals or reptiles?

Answer on page 278

Star track

Put a number in each empty circle so that each straight line adds up to 25.

9

3 9

5 6

5 8

5

Answer on page 278

I Spy sea creatures

Look at the picture carefully.
How many sea creatures can you find?

I found ___ sea creatures. They are: ________________

____

Answer on page 278

Color fun

Color in the barbecue scene.

What is your favorite barbecue food?

I like ______________________________

Treasure hunt

To open the treasure chest the pirates have to find the numbers that can be divided exactly by 2. Can you help them? Start on number 6 and move from number to number – down or sideways to reach the bottom line and get the treasure.

6	8	2	12	11	9
9	13	15	2	4	7
11	5	9	7	16	2
3	1	14	20	18	1
16	4	17	4	9	3

Answer on page 278

Treasure hunt

Find the city

Rachel is going on vacation. Can you rearrange the letters to help her choose which city to visit?

ROYWNEK
____

ASRPI
____

OLDNNO
____

CSOMOW
____

REBNIL
____

Answer on page 278

Go on then!

Can you work out the joke?

EMRF SVS FMW QGY DRY FG FMW TAGO?

1 F	2 Z	3 I	4 E	5 N
8 D	9 A	10 B	11 C	6 G
7 M	12 L	Y	12 K	7 H
6 O	11 P	10 Q	9 R	8 S
5 X	4 W	3 V	2 U	1 T

MGC VF!

Answer on page 278

Geography lesson

Teacher: Ronald, can you tell me where the Andes are?

Ronald: At the end of your wristies?

Words and pictures

Can you draw a line to connect the different buildings with their names?

Answer on page 278

Fun quiz

Tick (✓) the correct answers.

1 What is the capital of the FRANCE?

Madrid ☐
Paris ☐
Washington ☐

2 Which one is not a fruit?

tomato ☐
onion ☐
apple ☐

3 Who is not an actor?

Pete Sampras ☐
Brad Pitt ☐
Sharon Stone ☐

Answer on page 279

Who is out there?

Connect the dots to find who is visiting earth. Then color in the creature.

Who is out there?

Follow the shortest path in the forest. The letters spread on the route will help you spell the name of an animal.

Answer on page 279

Too sweet for you

Can you work out how many chocolates are left in each box?

____Chocolates left

____Chocolates left

____Chocolates left

____Chocolates left

Answer on page 279

Sea sighed

What does the sea say to the beach?

Not much it mostly just waves.

I Spy

Find and circle all the pyramids.

Answer on page 279

Color fun

Color the picture with pencils, paints or crayons.

Space search

Can you find and circle 9 space words?

A	V	C	B	K	S	P
S	P	E	N	O	S	L
P	L	A	N	E	T	U
M	A	R	S	U	N	T
O	S	T	A	R	S	O
O	K	H	W	S	S	J
N	S	A	T	U	R	N

Answer on page 279

Spot the word

Write the first letter of each picture and rearrange them to spell a new word.

The new word is ____________________

Answer on page 279

Aztec

An ancient Indian god has sent a message to his followers carved in stone. What should the Indians watch out for?

The carved message reads ___________________________

Answer on page 279

Higher or hire?

How do you hire a taxi?

Put a brick under each wheel!

Matching pyramids

Draw a line to join the matching pyramids.

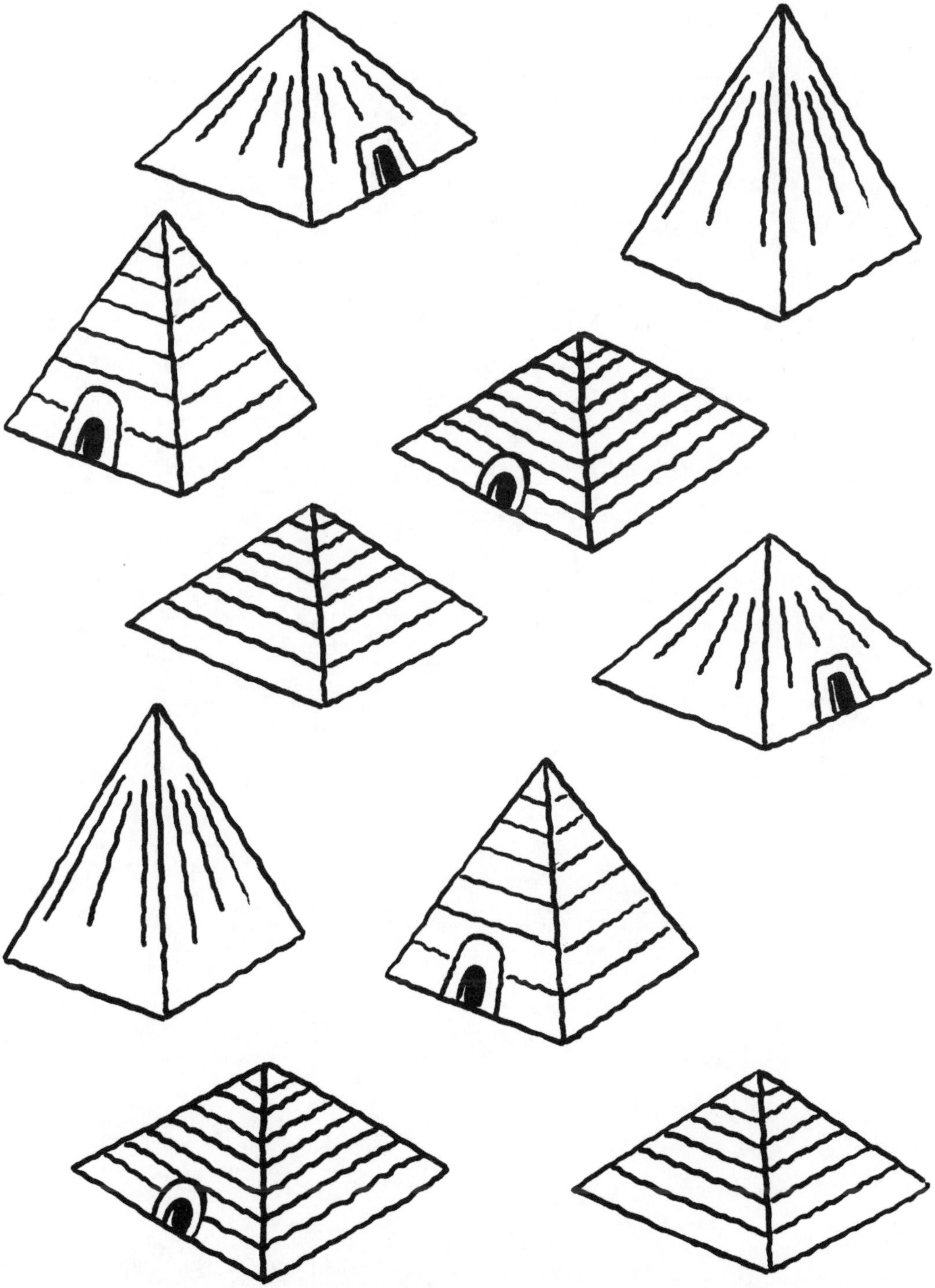

Answer on page 279

Fun quiz

Tick (✓) the correct answers.

1 Which of these colors is in the Spanish Flag?

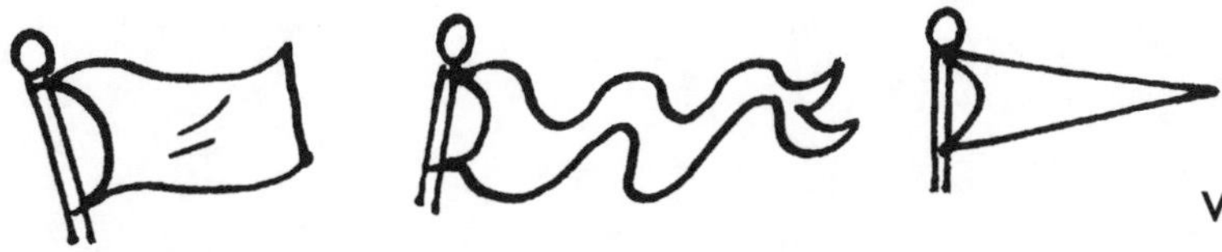

red ☐
blue ☐
white ☐

2 Which of these fruits grows on trees?

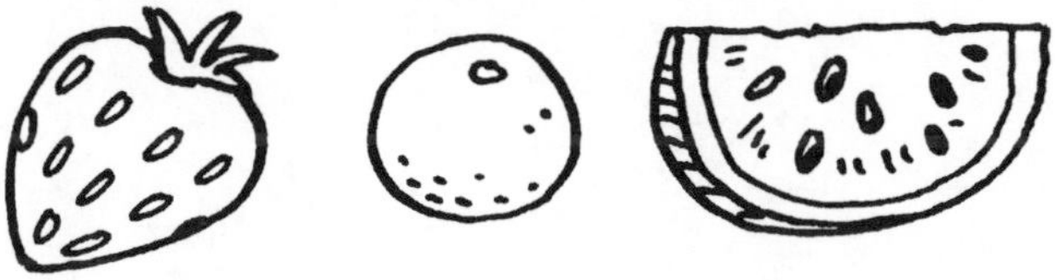

oranges ☐
watermelon ☐
strawberries ☐

3 Which of these animals has the longest neck?

hamster ☐
dog ☐
giraffe ☐

4 Which of these names is the odd one out?

Mary ☐
Edward ☐
Sarah ☐

5 What is the currency of France?

Rupee ☐
Franc ☐
Pound ☐

Answer on page 279

Connect the dots

Draw a line to connect the dots and find what is this girl's favorite activity.

Pirate's maze

Can you help Blackbeard find his lost treasure? He has to collect the key first!

Answer on page 280

Spycatcher

Can you decode the message to find out what the spy will be disguised as?

ETH YSP LWIL EB DDRESSE SA A NMILKMA

The spy will be disguised as ______________________

Answer on page 280

One track line

Draw a line to join the trains in numerical order. What do all the numbers add up to?

All the numbers add up to ____________

Answer on page 280

Hard-headed?

What do you call a man under a car?

Jack!

Spot the sun cream

How many tubes of sun cream can you spot in this picture? Find and circle them.

Answer on page 280

Half a zebra

Complete the picture and color it in.

Which animal, related to the zebra, can we ride?

Answer on page 280

187

Spycatcher

You suspect that a family member is a spy. Who could it be? Delete all the letters that appear twice to find the answer.

B	U	F	A	J	Y	D
Z	W	N	I	G	X	M
O	D	W	C	H	B	Z
K	Y	M	J	L	A	K
X	H	O	G	F	E	I

The spy is the ____________

Answer on page 280

Lined up

Can you find the names of 6 birds in the line below?

Answer on page 280

189

Lost in Egypt

The traveler has to work out the key to the map to find his oasis in the desert. Use the code shown.

The message says: ____

____

Answer on page 280

Off the menu

Why don't sharks eat penguins?

Because they find the wrappers difficult!

Matching pairs

Draw lines to match the flying saucers. Can you find the odd one out?

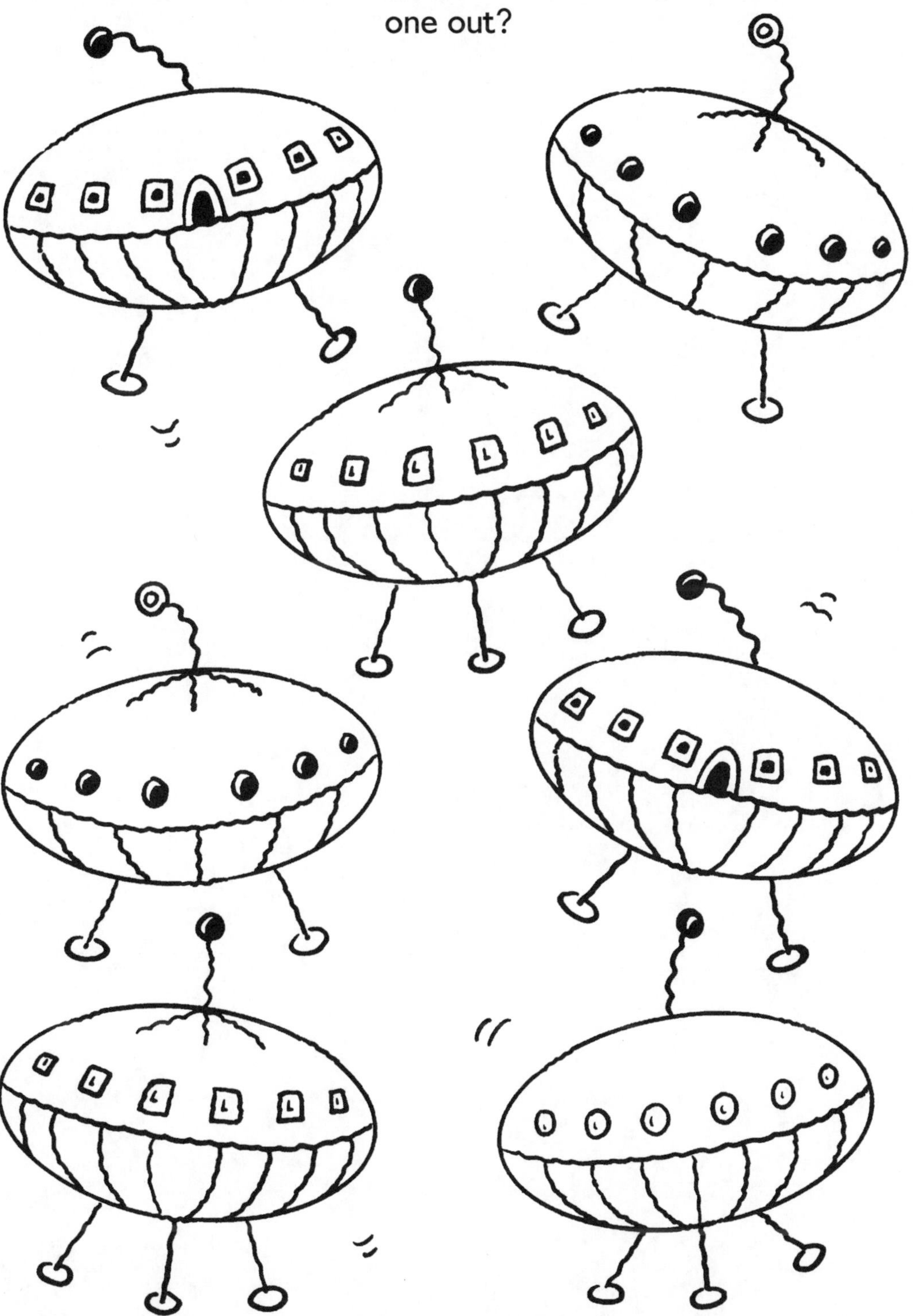

Answer on page 280

192

Lost in space rebus

A spaceship crashes with a message engraved on its front panel. Can you work out what it means?

The greeting from space is ________________

Answer on page 281

193

High Q

Of all the animals, which has the highest brain power?

The Giraffe!

Connect the dots to complete the picture.

Answer on page 281

To the airport

006 needs the shortest route to the airport avoiding all the road blocks. Can you help her?

Answer on page 281

Ready for tea

There were 3 sandwiches for each child. Can you find out how many sandwiches they have eaten already?

They have eaten ______ sandwiches.

Answer on page 281

Spot the sea creatures

There are 7 different sea creatures in this picture. Can you find and circle them?

The sea creatures are ______________________________

____

____

Answer on page 281

Beach wear

What sort of shoes do frogs wear on the beach?

Open toad sandals!

Moon walker

Use paints, pencils or crayons to color the astronaut.

When did the first man walk on the moon?

Answer on page 281

199

Detective wordsearch

Can you find 9 words to do with detectives? Circle them.

B	H	A	S	R	N	E	Y	S
A	I	N	E	D	F	R	P	C
I	D	E	C	N	N	Y	C	O
D	D	S	R	D	O	A	O	D
D	E	T	E	C	T	I	V	E
N	N	C	T	E	E	W	E	I
C	L	U	E	T	S	H	R	M
M	E	S	S	A	G	E	T	E

Answer on page 281

200

Puzzle fruits

The mystery fruit is spelt from the <u>missing</u> six letters of the alphabet.

The mystery fruit is ___________

Answer on page 281

201

Message in a bottle

Using the code on this page, decode the message in the bottle.

The message says ________________________________

____

Answer on page 282

Close eye-counter

Mommy, mommy how is it that kids call me four eyes?

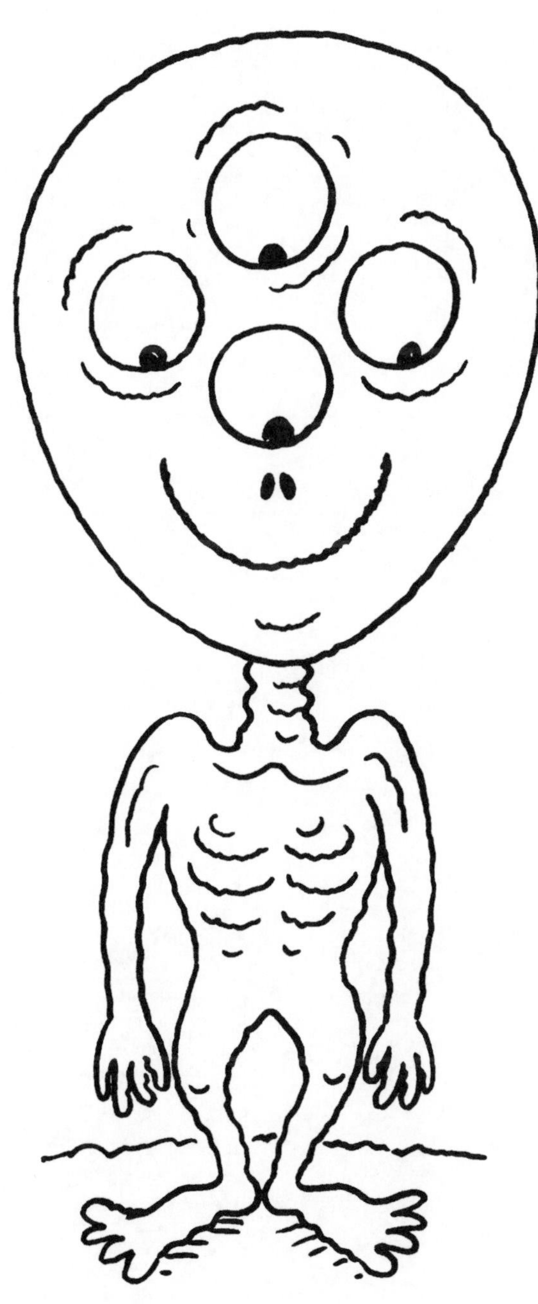

Eye, eye, eye, eye!

Tasty bites

There are seven names of foods in this picture that have been broken in two. Can you draw lines to connect them back together again?

The foods I found are __________, __________, __________, __________, __________, __________ and __________

Answer on page 282

Riddle

What gets wetter the more it dries?

A towel!

Crushing

What did the grape do when the elephant stood on it?

It just let out a little wine!

Connect the dots to complete the picture.

Answer on page 282

On the Nile

Which river should our explorer take of the three? Only one leads to safety. Can you help her find the correct river?

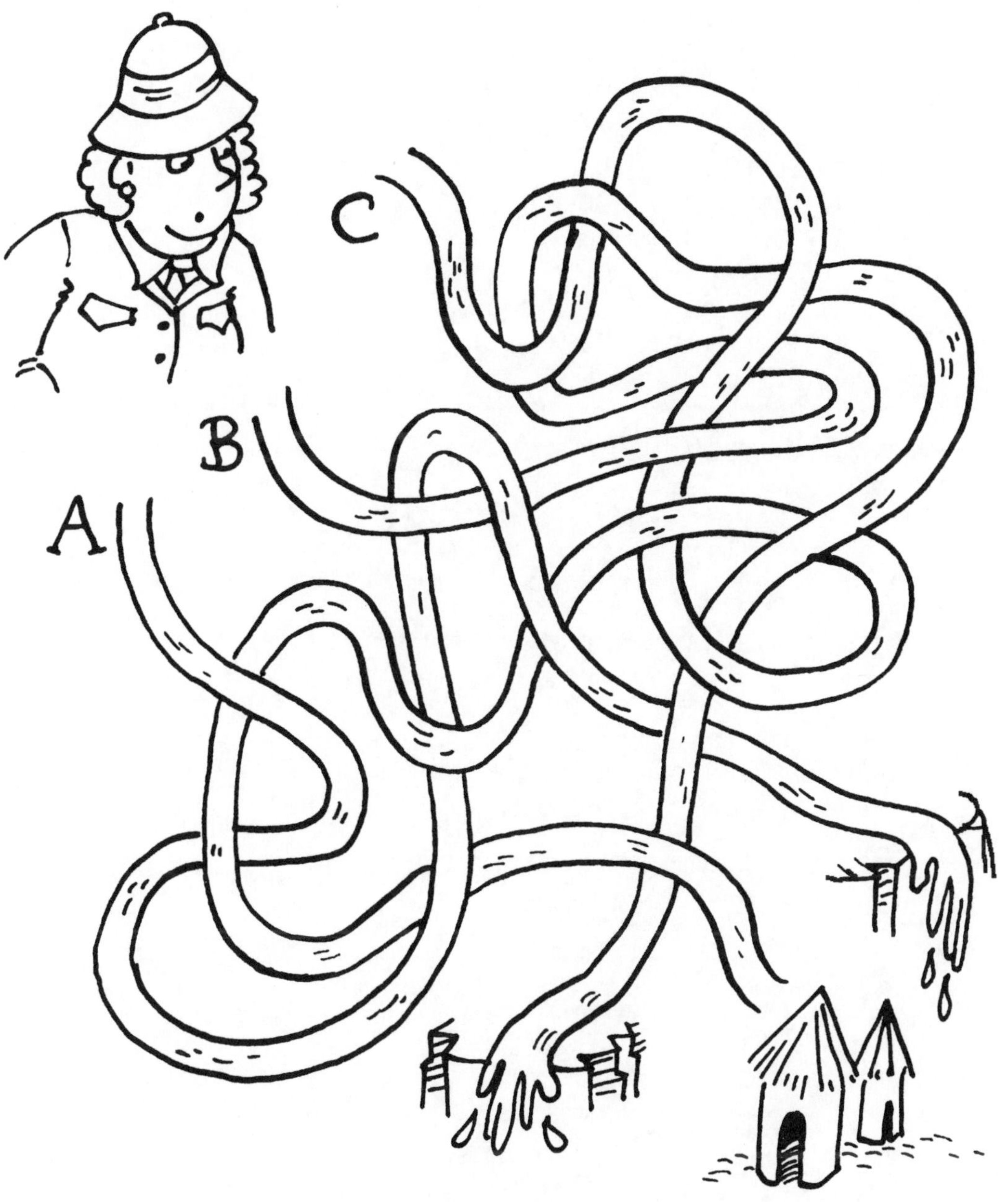

The river to choose is ______________

Answer on page 282

Anyone for tennis?

There were 10 tennis balls in each sportsbag. Can you find out how many are missing?

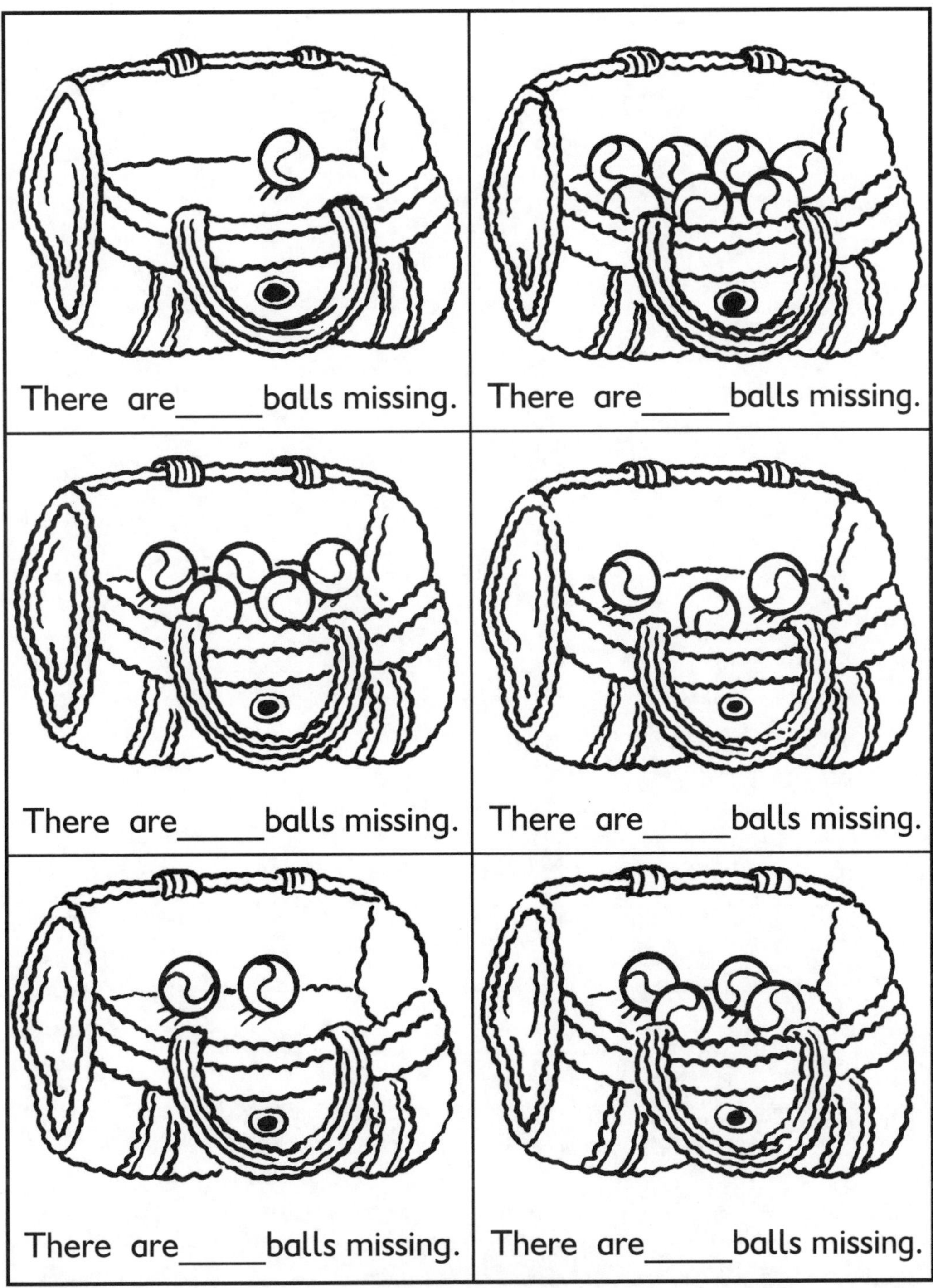
There are _____ balls missing.
There are _____ balls missing.
There are _____ balls missing.
There are _____ balls missing.
There are _____ balls missing.
There are _____ balls missing.

Answer on page 282

Mind your own business!

Knock-knock. Who's there? Scot. Scot who?

Scot nothing to do with you!

I Spy odd things

There are 6 odd things in the picture. Can you find them?

The odd things I found are: ______________________________

____

Answer on page 282

Color fun

Color in the elephant, the biggest land mammal in the world.

Do you know where elephants are found?

Answer on page 282

Wordsearch

Find and circle eight space words; they can go in any direction. Then use the leftover letters to make at least three new words.

M	A	R	S	Z	U	L	A	R
A	J	U	P	I	T	E	R	R
R	X	Y	A	S	P	T	O	N
T	G	G	C	A	T	X	C	E
I	O	U	E	N	Y	O	K	T
A	V	N	O	O	M	Z	E	N
N	F	B	P	E	Z	A	T	S
Y	A	G	T	P	E	F	N	T

The new words that I found are __________ __________

__________ and __________

Answer on page 282

Word gaps

Add one 3-letter word to each group to make longer words.

Group 1

_ _ _ TEN

T_ _ _ S

W_ _ _ E

Group 2

ST_ _ _ ER

_ _ _ IST

P_ _ _ ING

Group 3

CAR_ _ _

TRUM_ _ _

_ _ _ AL

Answer on page 283

Useful tales

What type of snakes can you find on cars?

Windscreen Vipers!

Word pairs

The name of each picture can be paired with another one to make a new word or phrase. Can you find them?

The new phrases/words are ______________________,

______________________,

and ______________________

Answer on page 283

Fun quiz

Three spies are trying to escape. Can you tell who is going to Australia?

________________ is going to Australia

Answer on page 283

It's not nice

Why do fishes go 'gloop, gloop'?

Because if they went 'Poop, Poop' it would be rude.

Connect the dots to complete the picture.

Answer on page 283

Aztec maze

Help Professor Xavier find the quickest route to the Aztec tomb.

Answer on page 283

More milk please

If the mommy cow can give 4 litres of milk a day and the young cow can give 3 litres, how many litres can the daddy cow give a day?

Answer on page 283

Clues

Dracula's mommy was murdered. Who investigated the crime?

Sherlock Bones!

I Spy ice

Find the complete ice creams in this picture and color them.

Answer on page 283

221

Spycatcher

Can you work out the names of the cities from these coded spy names by removing some letters as in the example?

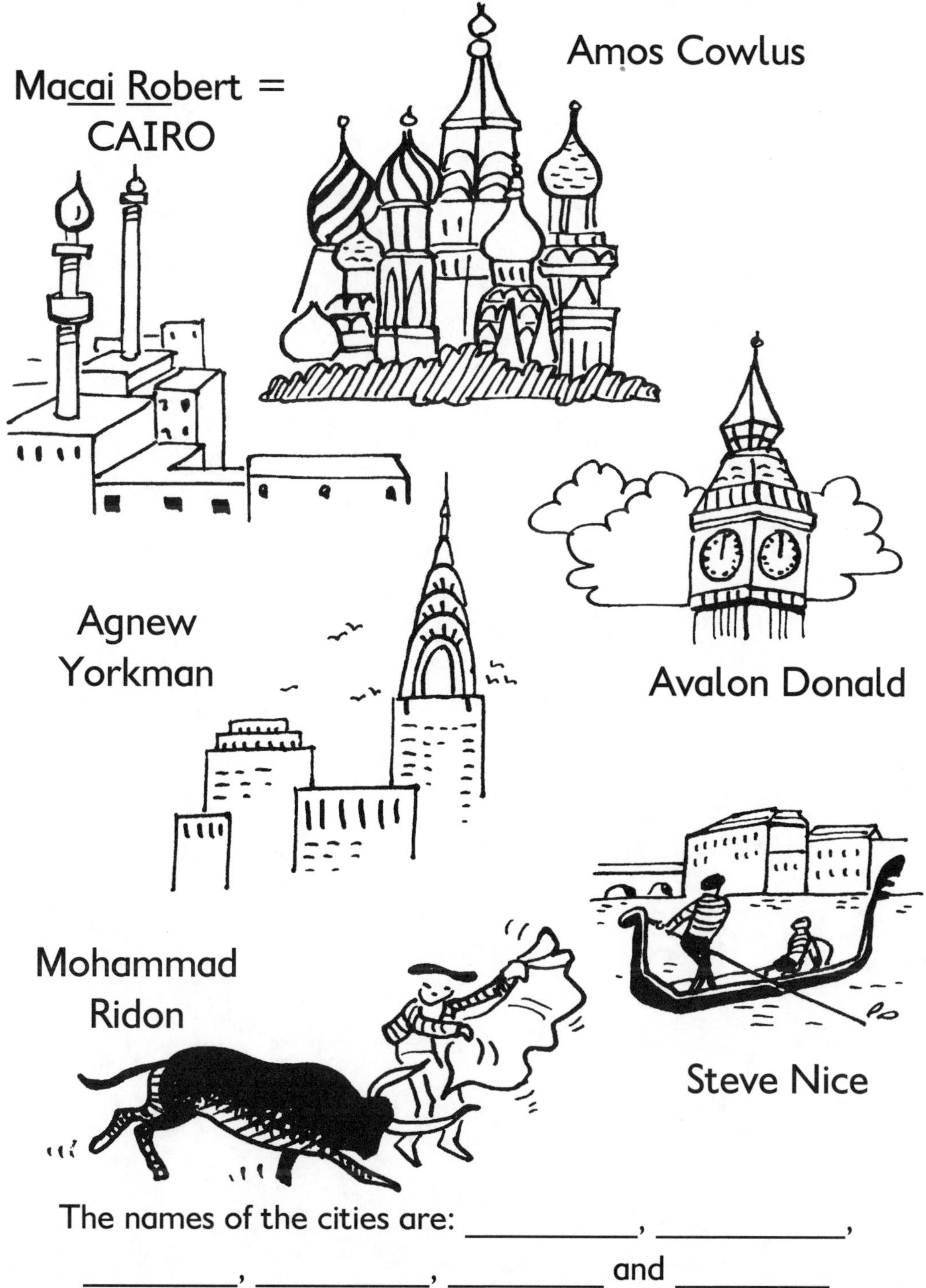

The names of the cities are: __________, __________,

__________, __________, __________ and __________

Answer on page 284

Complete the picture

Complete this half picture using the grid as a guide.
Then color it!

223

Lost words

Cross out the letters that appear twice in the grid and find out what is flying in the sky.

F	P	B	S	Z	S
K	L	G	O	J	D
Z	I	D	Y	R	Q
H	Q	T	H	A	L
N	A	B	E	P	R
G	N	O	J	Y	F

I looked in the sky. The flying object is a __________.

Answer on page 284

Bird anagrams

Can you rearrange these words so that they make sense?

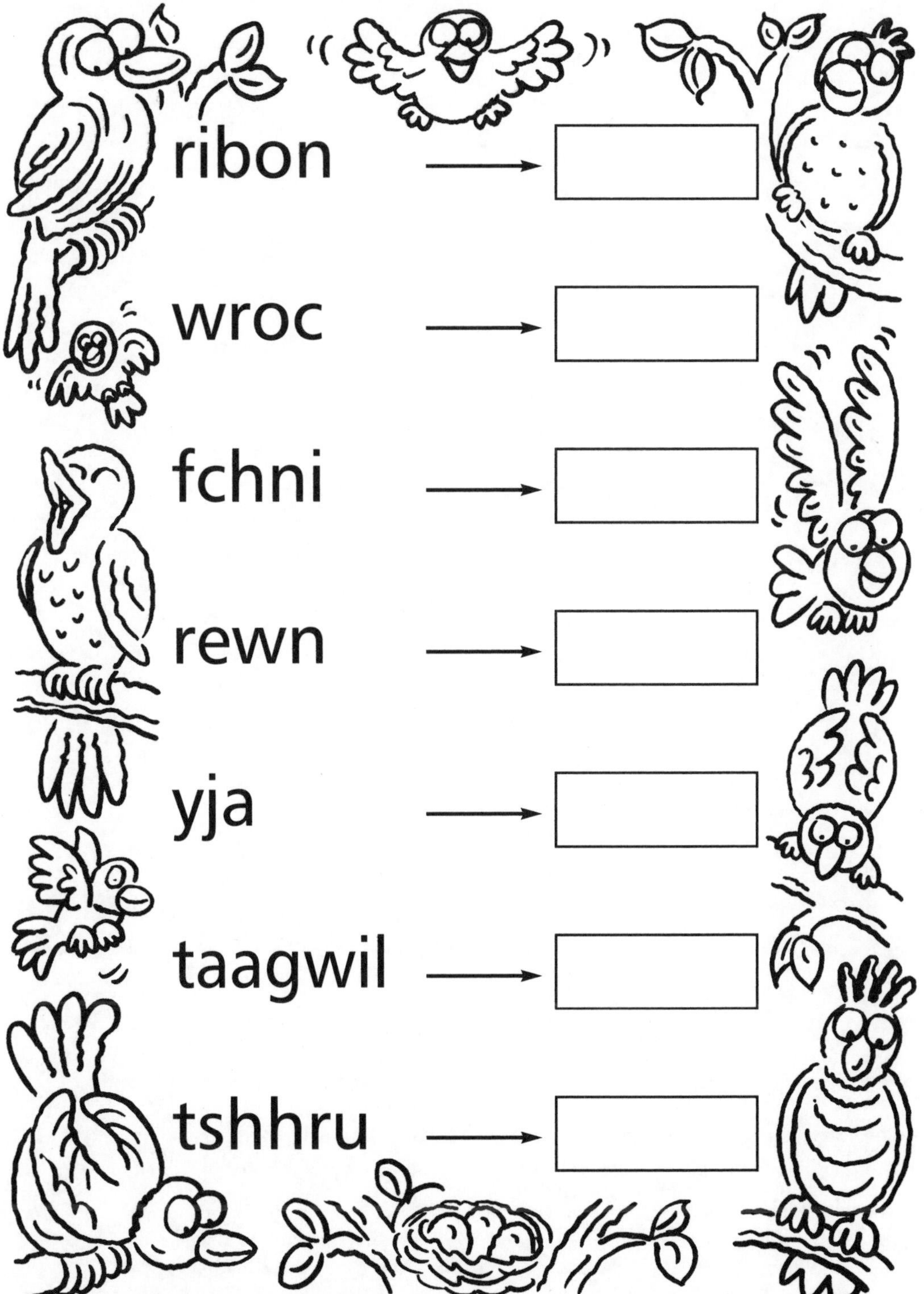

Answer on page 284

Pie in the sky

What do the children of Italy dream of eating?

The Leaning Tower of Pizza!

Word pairs

The name of each object can be paired with another one to make a new word or phrase. Can you find them?

The new words/phrases are ______________________,

______________________, and ______________________

Answer on page 284

Dotty cat

What is the cat in 'The Jungle Book' called?

Meowgli!

Connect the dots to complete the picture.

Answer on page 284

Escape maze

Which road should 007 take to get to the airport?

He should take road ________

Answer on page 284

Sea letters

How many letter o's can you spot in this picture? Don't count the eyes as they are ovals.

I spotted ______ 'o's

Answer on page 284

Geography lesson

What is the capital of Italy?

'I'

I Spied a spider

What has eight legs and flies?

A spider in an airplane.

Coded picture

Rearrange the picture to find out what the spy is doing.

Answer on page 285

233

Lost words

Cross out the letters that appear twice in the grid and find the hiding sea creature.

D	L	G	F	I	O
U	C	K	P	J	S
E	F	R	A	X	E
J	P	D	X	B	U
S	I	O	G	K	L

I found the creature. It is a ________

Answer on page 285

Vacation signs

This signpost points to six different countries. Can you unscramble their names?

The six countries are __________, ______________,

______________, ______________,

______________ and ___________

Answer on page 285

Favorites

What is Dracula's favorite TV program?

Bat Watch!

Pictures and letters

These pictures begin with different letters. Draw lines to join the correct letters to the correct pictures.

Answer on page 285

Flying tonight?

Who were the first brothers not to invent the airplane?

The WRONG brothers.

Connect the dots to complete the picture.

Answer on page 285

Spy words anagram

Can you unscramble these words? They all have something to do with spies.

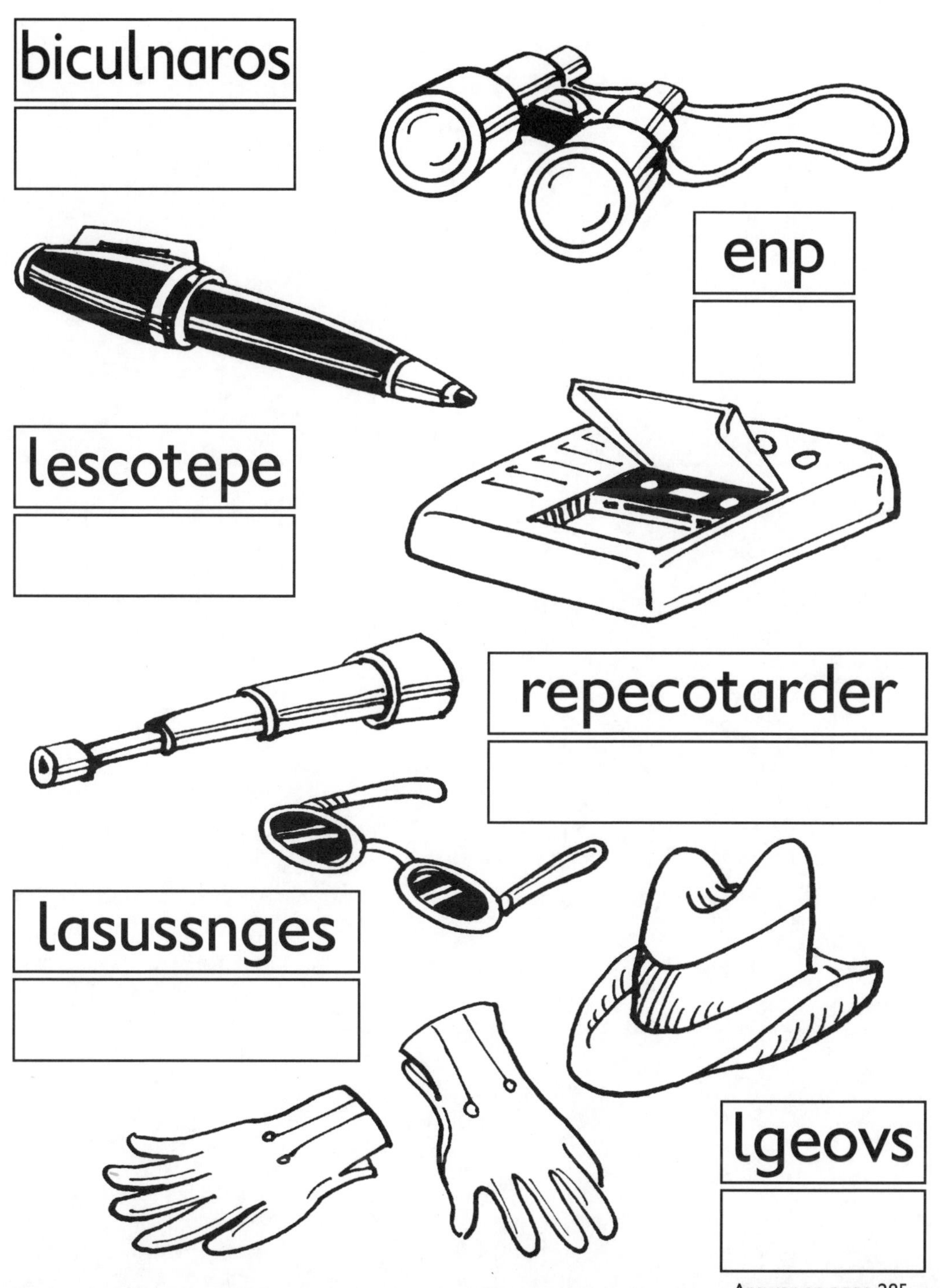

Answer on page 285

Convenient

Why did the Zombie move into the morgue?

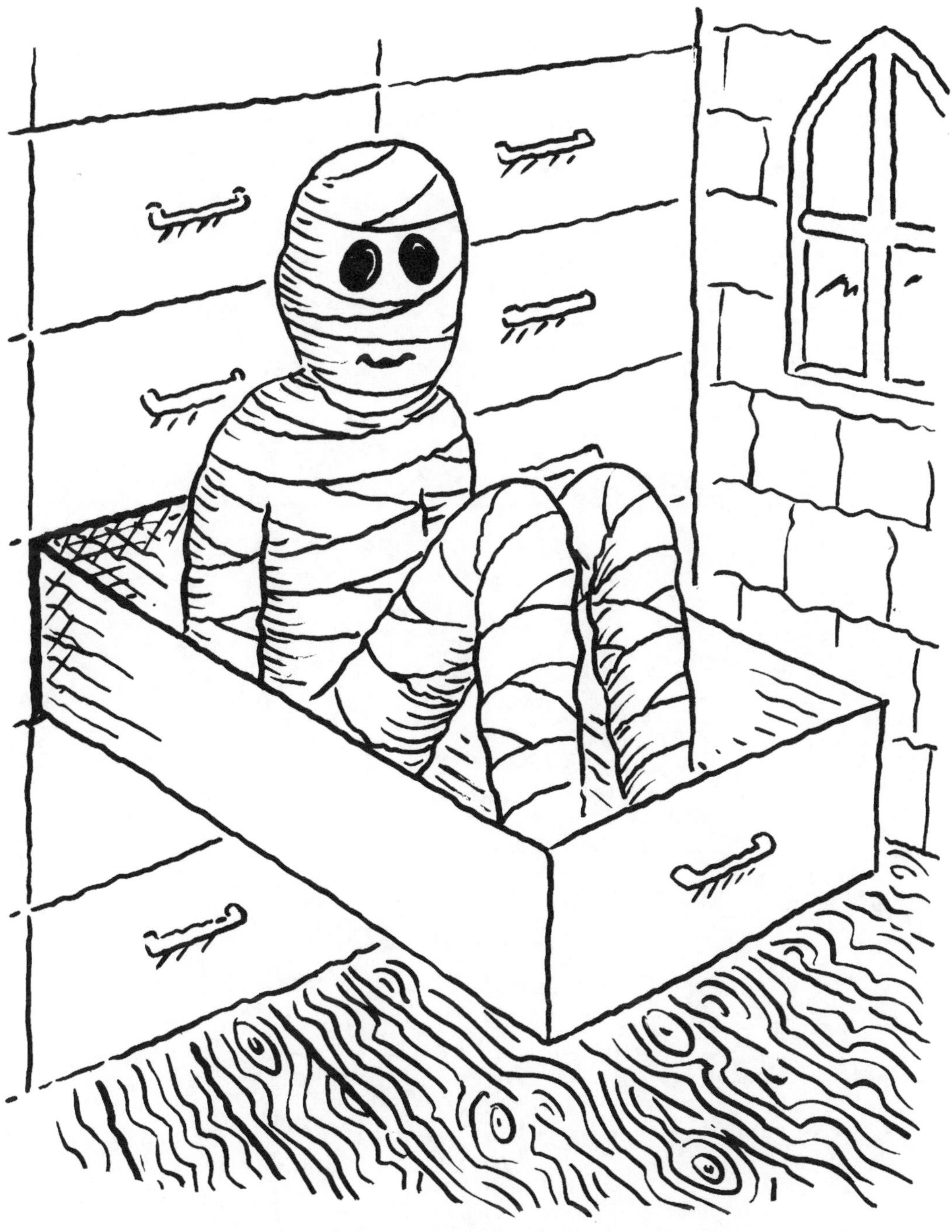

Because it was the dead center of town!

Circle it

Look at the picture carefully. How many complete circles can you find?

I found ________ circles.

Answer on page 285

I Spy

Can you spot six things that begin with the letter **a**?

I found __________, __________, __________,

__________, __________ and __________

Answer on page 285

Chicken

Why did the chewing gum cross the road?

It was stuck to the chicken's foot.

243

Suitcase wordsearch

The suitcase is ready. Can you find 8 items that the young girl will take with her?

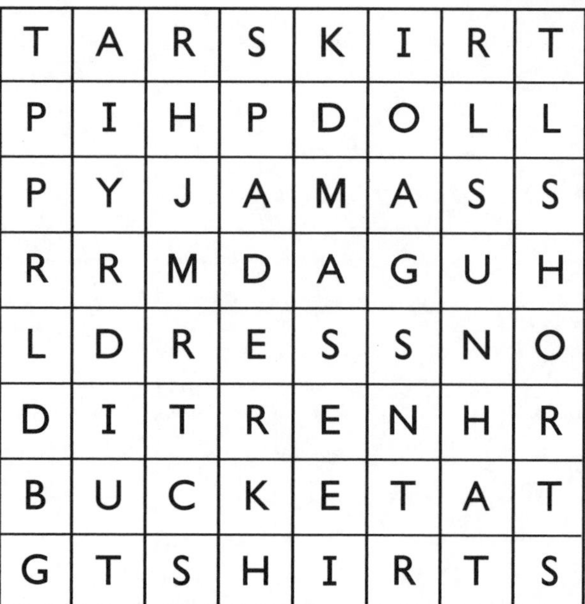

T	A	R	S	K	I	R	T
P	I	H	P	D	O	L	L
P	Y	J	A	M	A	S	S
R	R	M	D	A	G	U	H
L	D	R	E	S	S	N	O
D	I	T	R	E	N	H	R
B	U	C	K	E	T	A	T
G	T	S	H	I	R	T	S

Answer on page 286

Games and sports

Can you rearrange the words to spell five sports?

nnetsi →

kcricet →

logf →

simingmw →

sngilai →

The five sports are: ________________,

________________, ________________,

________________ and ________________

Answer on page 286

Brain teaser

What is the last thing to pass through a fly's mind as it crashes into a windscreen?

Its bottom!

Matching pairs

Draw lines to connect the pairs of hats.

Answer on page 286

Police hideout

Connect the dots to find out where the chief of police is having a break from criminals.

Answer on page 286

How many?

How many different types of fruit can you find in this picture?
Can you count them?

I found ____

____

Answer on page 286

I Spy D's

There are seven things beginning with D in this picture. Can you find them?

I found ________________, ________________,

________________, ________________, ________________

________________________ and ________________

Answer on page 286

Petsearch

Can you find how many pets Peter's family are leaving for Grandma to look after when they go on vacation? One doesn't show itself.

FROG

RABBIT

R	A	B	B	I	T
P	I	H	Z	F	O
Q	W	A	T	R	A
R	R	M	D	O	G
L	N	S	U	G	X
C	A	T	R	I	N
K	E	E	L	J	V
G	E	R	B	I	L

CAT

DOG

GERBIL

Answer on page 286

Anagrams

Can you sort out these six mixed-up words? The pictures may help you to work them out.

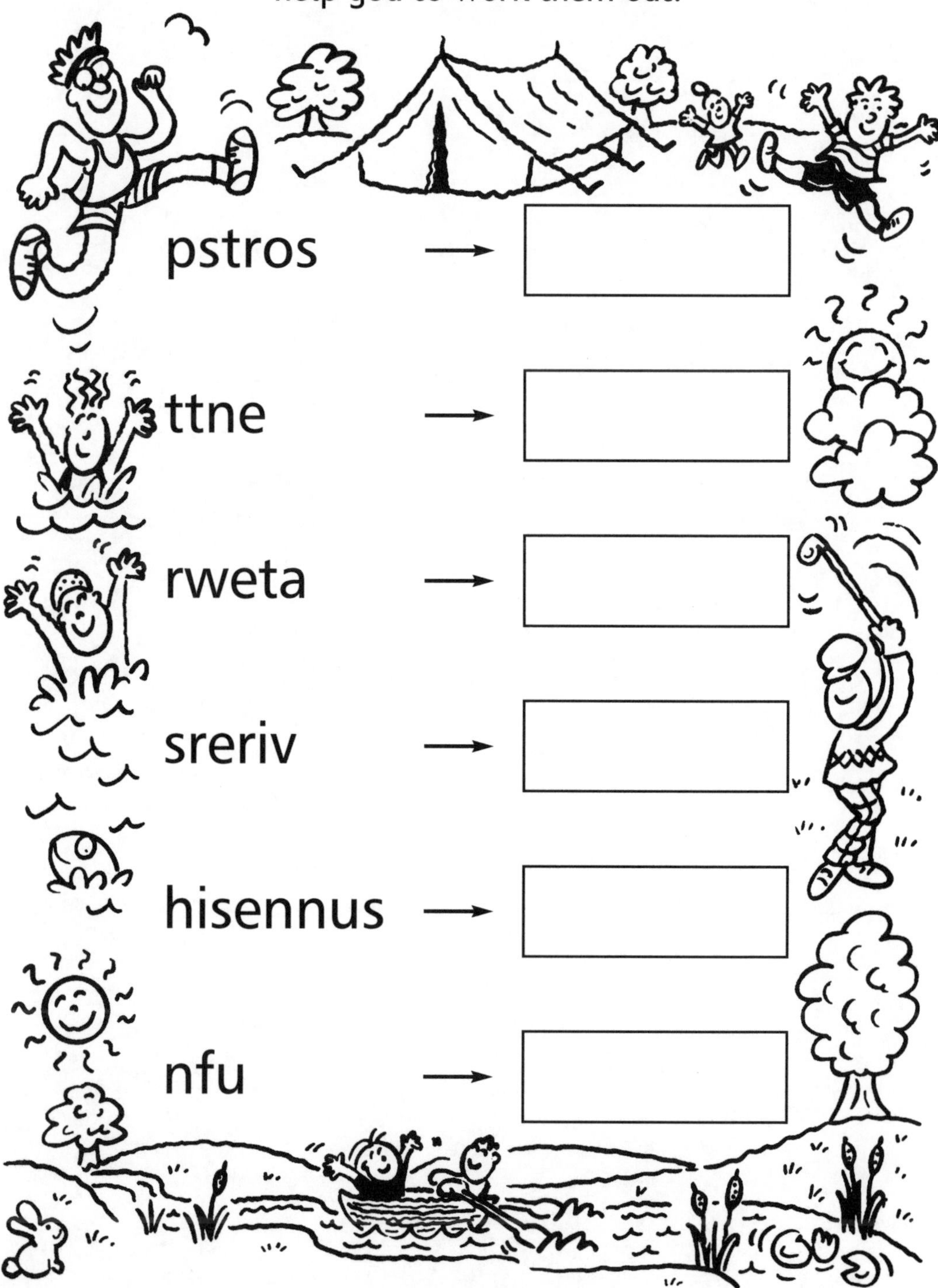

pstros →

ttne →

rweta →

sreriv →

hisennus →

nfu →

Answer on page 286

Cow tale

Where do cowboys get their cows?

MOO YORK!

Matching pairs

Which of these things rhyme? Draw lines to connect the pairs of rhyming things.

Answer on page 286

Spycatcher

The secret location where the spies will meet next is written in this letter. Can you find it? Try taking one word from each sentence to make a new sentence.

See, it is important to
take care. You need
string and matches. In
the morning buy a
newspaper. The best
is the Daily Bugle.
Toy monkeys can hide
the secrets. Shop for
some apples, try to
look normal.

The letter contains this message ________________________

____

Answer on page 287

Connect the dots

connect the dots to see 007's vacation home.

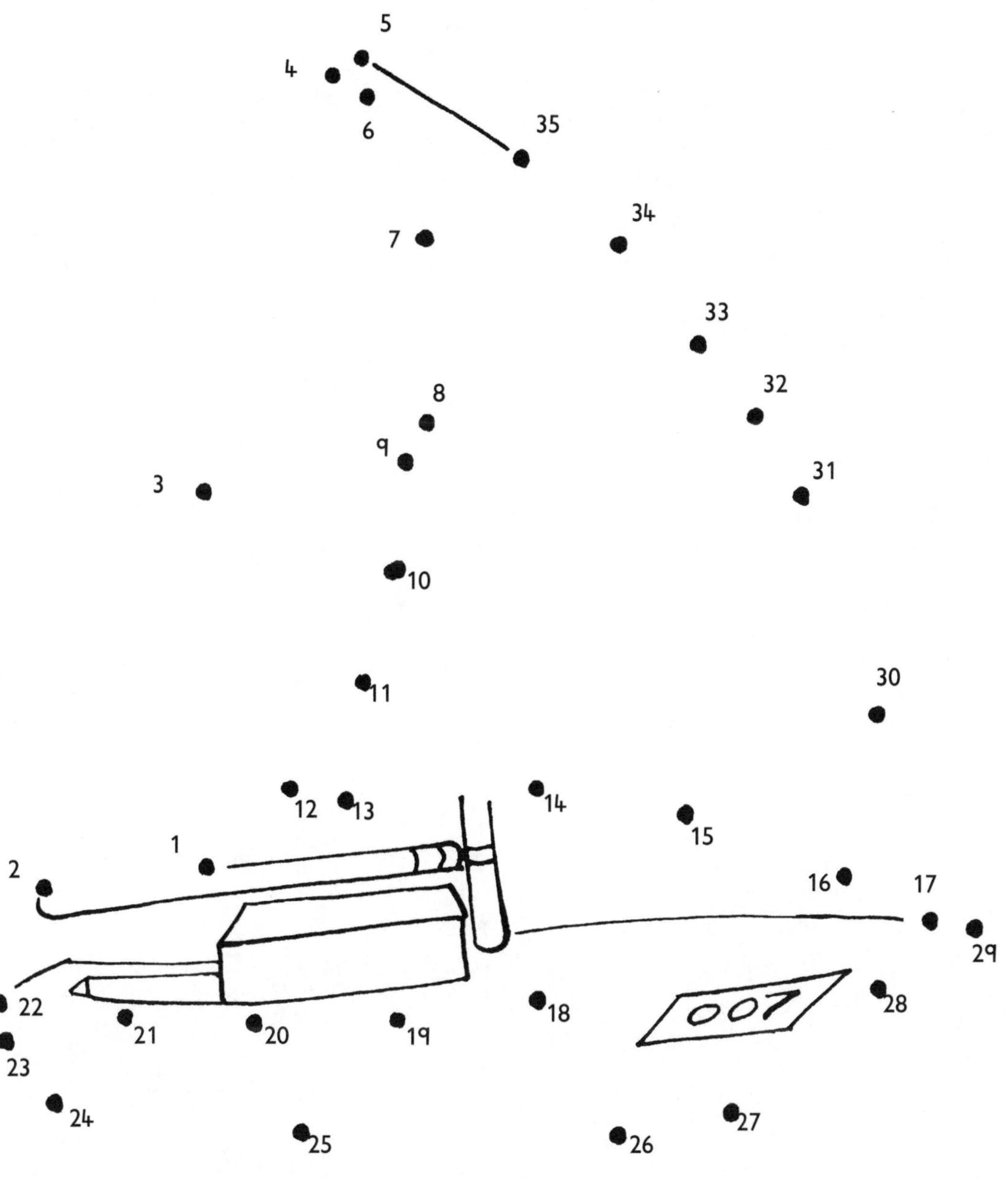

Answer on page 287

Webby funny

What is a spy with 8 legs called?

A SPY-DER! (spider)

Travel search

There are 10 words hidden in this puzzle that are about travel. Can you find them all? The pictures may help you. Remember the words can go in any direction.

T	F	P	T	H	R	V	U	G	T
H	T	G	L	G	C	A	R	F	E
R	L	H	T	A	M	N	T	O	L
B	I	K	E	T	N	G	U	C	O
U	N	T	O	A	O	E	R	Z	R
H	E	L	I	C	O	P	T	E	R
H	R	F	Z	O	T	P	R	E	Y
T	O	R	N	A	D	B	U	S	N
I	B	H	M	C	I	Z	C	Z	E
Y	T	O	W	H	L	Q	K	R	R

Answer on page 287

Broken words

Six names of things often found in the countryside have broken up into pieces. Can you join them back together again?

The six words are: ______________, ______________,

______________, ______________

______________ and ______________

Answer on page 287

Dotty detective

Connect the dots to find out who the detective is.

Answer on page 287

Spycatcher

The name of the friend of a spy is in this message. Can you read it?

MORE INSECTS SEE
SOME MONKEYS
OR NEWTS
EVERY YEAR
PERHAPS EVEN
NAUGHTY NEWTS
YELLING

The spy's friend is ____________________________

Answer on page 287

Sick teacher

Did you hear about the mathematics teacher who came over all faint?

Everyone tried to bring him 2!

Wordsearch

Circle the 7 number words.

E	V	C	B	F	Y	T
I	L	O	L	I	S	W
G	J	E	I	V	W	E
H	S	E	V	E	N	L
T	E	N	W	E	M	V
B	A	J	C	O	N	E

Answer on page 287

Answers (are only given if not obvious from the page)

Page

1 **Matching pairs:** the odd bus out is number 10

3 **Fun puzzler:** there are 10 cows and 20 hens (heads and legs of COWS=50, heads and legs of CHICKENS= 60, 110 in all)

4 **Connect the dots:** the picture is of a ROLLER COASTER. It can be found in a FUNFAIR or ADVENTURE PARK

5 **Monkey maze:** path E has 9 BANANAS

7 **Odd one out:** the BANANA is the odd one out as all the others are ROUND (the mushroom has a round cap)

9 **Squirrels high and low:** 6, 8, 11, 12, 15, 17 and 19

Page

10 **Vacation horror:** TRAINS can give you STRAIN

12 **Fair crossword:** Across: 1 ICES, 2 POPCORN, Down: 1 CHIPS, 2 OPEN, 3 DARTS

13 **Broken words:** the words are GIRAFFE, HORSE, ELEPHANT, DUCK, CHICKEN and FROG

14 **No joke:** WHERE DOES KING KONG SLEEP? – ANYWHERE HE WANTS TO

Answers

Page		Page	

15 **Spot the differences:**

16 **Pharaoh's curse:** the message for the professor reads SHAVE YOUR HEAD NOW

18 **Matching pairs:** the matching sand castle and flags are 9 and 11-2, 4 and 13-9, 7 and 15-8, 11 and 14-3, 5 and 20-15, 15 and 20-5, 3 and 19-16

19 **Fun quiz:** a baby elephant is called a CALF

20 **Connect the dots:** the picture is of a SPACESHIP

21 **Amazing:** path A leads to house 3.

24 **Odd one out:** the odd one out is the HAT because all the others start with the letter S

25 **Color fun:** the matching doors and windows are 16 and 19-3, 13 and 18-5, 15 and 16-1, 19 and 20-1 and 10 and 11-1

Answers

Page

26 **Spot the differences:**

27 **Space word wheel:**

Page

28 **Crossword:** the words are: Across – 1 BOAT, 2 FISH, 3 TREASURE Down – 1 ANCHOR, 2 RING, 3 SHARK, 4 EEL

30 **Speedy?** the quicker ones are – the CAR, the PLANE, the TRAIN and the ROCKET

31 **Fun quiz:** the animals that live along the river bank are the VOLE and the WATER-RAT

32 **Connect the dots:** the picture is of a HOT-AIR BALLOON

33 **Picture this:** the spy is picture B

36 **Odd one out:** the odd bird out is the OSTRICH because it cannot fly. The other three birds can fly

Answers

Page		Page	

38 **Spot the differences:**

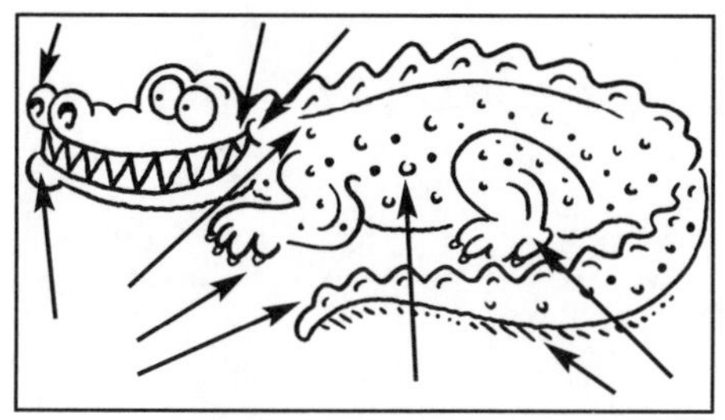

39 **Help:** the Egyptian says HAS ANYONE SEEN MY MUMMY?

40 **Crossword:** the words are: Across – 1 PETROL, 2 WHEEL, 3 PEDALS, 4 MIRROR, Down – 1 TYRE, 2 WIPER, 3 OIL

42 **Matching pairs:** train number 3 is the odd one out

43 **Fun quiz:** Italy belongs to EUROPE

44 **Connect the dots:** the picture is of a TREASURE CHEST

45 **Spy maze:** the word is HOSTAGE

47 **Odd one out:** the BEAN which is a vegetable, is the odd one out; all the others are fruits

49 **Spot the differences:**

50 **Holiday word wheel:** the new words are FRYING PAN

51 **Cross word?** the words are: Across – 1 ANNOYED, 2 WILD, Down – 1 HAPPY, 2 ANGRY, 3 FIERCE, 4 DOWN and 5 SAD

53 **Heavier or lighter:** the heavier ones are the PLANE, the TRAIN and the LINER

Answers

Page		Page	
54	**Fun quiz:** road B	61	**Spot the differences:**
55	**Connect the dots:** the picture is of a BOAT. Other words could be SHIP or LINER	62	**Summertime word wheel:** the word is ROSEBUSH
56	**Agent's maze:** path number 1 links the two secret agents		
57	**Count the fish:** ELEVEN FISH are staying.		
59	**Odd one out**: this is the MICROPHONE as all the others help with SEEING not HEARING/SPEAKING		
60	**Fly a kite:** the kites are 11+14, 10+15, 9+16, 12+13, 16+9, 17+8 and 19+6		

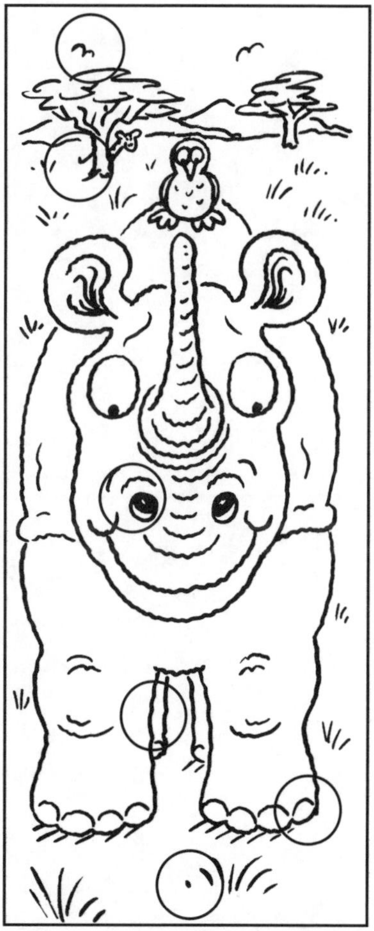

Answers

Page

63 **Pirate's dream:** the hidden word in the middle column is TREASURE

65 **Fishing:**

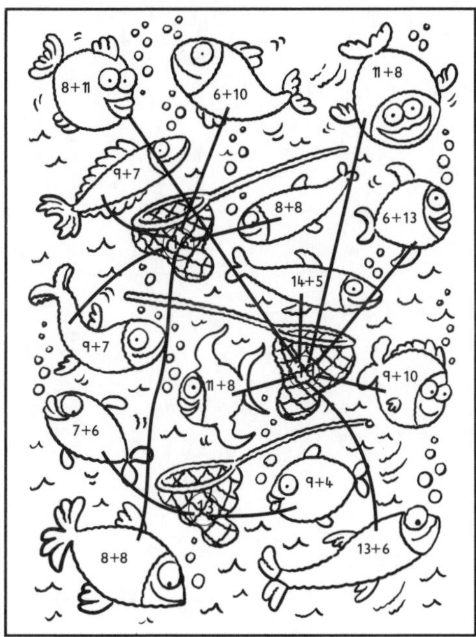

66 **Fun quiz:** six boys will eat 18 PIZZAS in 6 days

67 **Connect the dots:** the picture shows a DODGEM car in a funfair

Page

68 **Amazing:**

69 **Count the triangles:** there are FOURTEEN triangles

70 **Odd ones out:** they are middle house, boat on right, train bottom left

72 **What's the name?** the name is CLEOPATRA

Answers

Page	
73	**Diamonds are forever:** the secret word is JEWEL
75	**Spot the differences:** the differences are 1 broken AERIAL, 2 FRONT LIGHT missing, 3 WING MIRROR missing, 4 SUN ROOF missing, 5 MACHINE GUN missing, 6 CAR BADGE missing from hood
76	**Word wheel:** the phrase is ROCK POOL

Page	
77	**Cold and stranded:** ICE (1 PICK, 2 CROC, 3 SEED)
79	**Finishing order:** the cars finish in this order 20, 19, 18, 17, 16, 15 and last 14
80	**Fun quiz:** the ROBIN is the smallest
81	**Connect the dots:** the picture is of an OCTOPUS
82	**Amazing:**

Answers

Page		Page	
83	**Dinner time:** the number missing from each bunch is (clockwise from top) 9, 14, 8, 12, 0 and 8 bananas	87	**In the deep deep forest:** the five mistakes are 1 a WINE GLASS in a tree, 2 a SEAL on the grass, 3 a small UMBRELLA with the mushrooms, 4 a FISH hiding in roots of tree and 5 a HEDGEHOG in a tree
85	**Odd bird out**: the ROBIN is the odd one out as it can fly; all the others cannot	88	**Anagram:** the words are CODE, MAGNIFYING, GLASS, HIDDEN, CLUE, SECRET
86	**Sunny days:**	89	**Mirror writing:** the message is MEET MY ASSISTANT AT JOEY'S SCRAPYARD WITH THE MONEY
		91	**Message in a bottle:** the message says DO NOT DROP LITTER
		92	**Seaside chain words:** the words are 1 SAND, 2 DONKEY, 3 YACHT, 4 TEAS, 5 SANDWICH

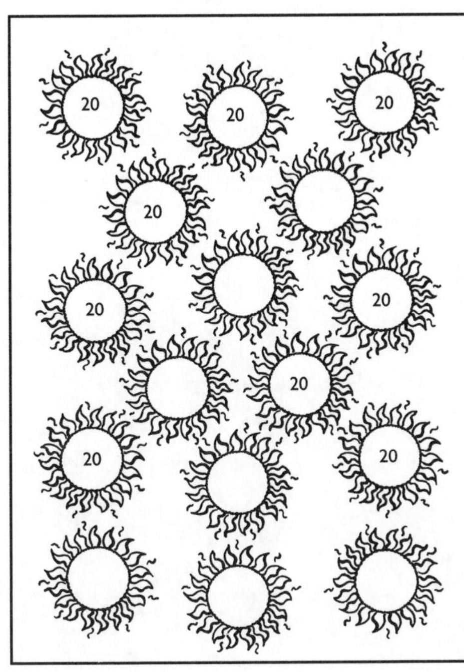

Answers

Page

93 **Butterfly beauties:**

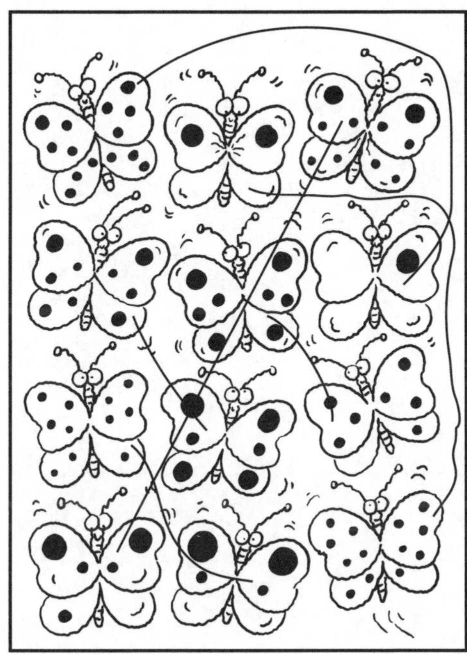

94 **Fun puzzle:** piece 1 and D, 2 and A, 3 and B, 4 and C, 5 and E

96 **Amazing:** the very hot boy can find his ICE by following the string B

97 **Spot the spots:** from top to bottom the numbers are: 3, 10, 2, 5, 7, 1, 8, 9, 0 and 4

Page

98 **Odd one out**: the odd one out is RIDE. All the others can form pairs that sound the same – FIR and FUR, HARE and HAIR, PAIR and PEAR, RODE and ROAD, TEAR and TARE

99 **Fireworks:**

Answers

Page

100 **Coastal errors:** SNOWMAN, CAR in sea, MOON, BOOK and SAND CASTLE upside down, LEGS missing from crab, COIN on rock, no stand for SUN UMBRELLA

101 **Word wheel:** the summer activity is SWIMMING

102 **Message in the tomb:** the message reads PULL THE RECTANGULAR STONE

104 **Sharing:** 5 and 9 NUTS

105 **Fun quiz**: the girl's name is INGRID

107 **Amazing:** the boy will stay in the CARAVAN

108 **Amazing:** the girl is going by SHIP

Page

109 **How many orders?** 19+2 and 21, 18+4 and 22, 17+6 and 23

110 **Odd one out:** the odd one out is MINE. All the others can be paired so that the pairs sound the same.

112 **Silly errors:** 1 WING on the plane is missing, 2 PYLON upside down, 3 number 3 on the 30 sign reversed, 4 CHIMNEY upside down, 5 SHADOW from road sign in wrong direction

113 **Word wheel:** the summer drink is LEMONADE

Answers

Page

114 Pirate's code: the grids should be like this

X	0	1	2	3	4	5
0	0	0	0	0	0	0
1	0	1	2	3	4	5
2	0	2	4	6	8	10
3	0	3	6	9	12	15

+	0	1	2	3	4	5	6	7
0	0	1	2	3	4	5	6	7
1	1	2	3	4	5	6	7	8
2	2	3	4	5	6	7	8	9
3	3	4	5	6	7	8	9	10
4	4	5	6	7	8	9	10	11

116 Matching pairs: the bathing suits match up like this

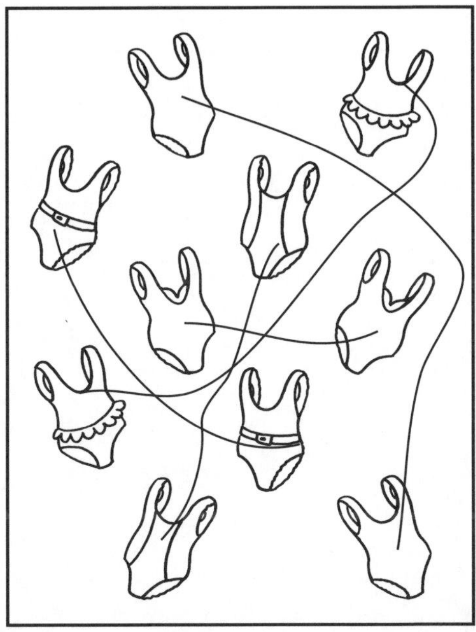

Page

117 Fun quiz: a ton of FEATHERS and a ton of LEAD weigh the SAME

118 Spooky connect the dots:

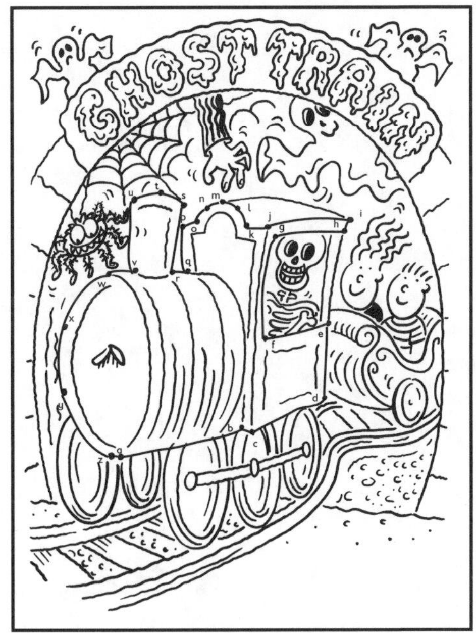

119 Anagram: the scrambled words are ESPIONAGE, CLUE, FLOWER, CHILD, CODE, SLEUTH, and COW

120 Invitations: follow this order 1,2,4,6,3,7 and 5

Answers

Page

121 **Strained?** The spycatcher is angry because HE MISSED THE TRAIN

122 **Countdown:** from top to bottom these are the days left 8, 23, 17 and 9

124 **Odd one out:** the odd one out is the SNOWMAN because all the others are about the summer

126 **Lost letters:** the eight lost letters are: A, C, F, G, W, V, X and Y

127 **Find the city:** the names of the cities are PARIS, MILAN, ATHENS, MADRID and OSLO

128 **Hidden meaning:** the words are THE PENTAGON

Page

130 **Words and pictures:**

131 **Fun quiz:** the GIRAFFE is the tallest

132 **Connect the dots:** the picture shows a man fishing

Answers

Page

133 The Marathon maze: this is the way through

134 Adding up: 50-30, 49-29, 34-14, 40-20 and 41-21

135 They nose! The note says YOU HAVE BEEN FOLLOWED, THEY KNOW YOU HAVE A FALSE NOSE!

137 Rhyming pairs: SOAP and ROPE, PAIL and MAIL, MUG and JUG, COAT and BOAT

Page

138 Color fun: there are 94 spots on the cheetah, this only includes those on the body - not the face

139 Surfing silly errors: the errors are 1 FISH instead of SUN, 2 TREE in the sea, 3 two people on one SURFBOARD, 4 boy surfing on IRONING BOARD 5 swimming HEDGEHOGS

140 How many words? you can make lots of words from HIPPOPOTAMUS. However many you made well done! Here are some you might have got HIP, POT, POP, AT, US, PAT, MAT, HAT, PIT, HIT, HOT, SHIP, SHOT, SHUT and SHOP

Answers

Page

141 **Spycatcher:** the message reads DO NOT COME TO OUR MEETING. I AM FOLLOWED

143 **Matching pairs**: the airplanes match up like this

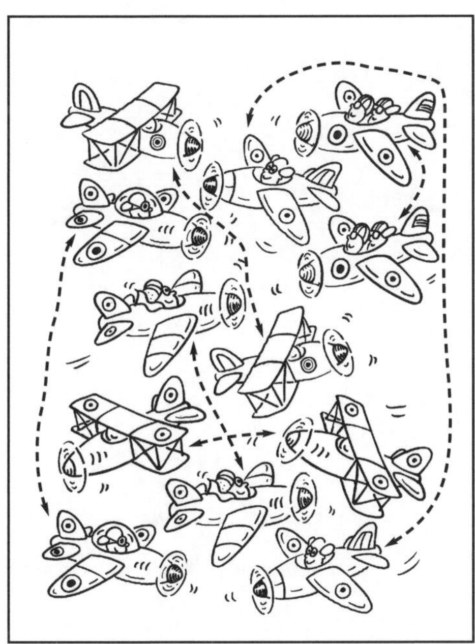

Page

144 **Fun puzzle**: the snake should look like this

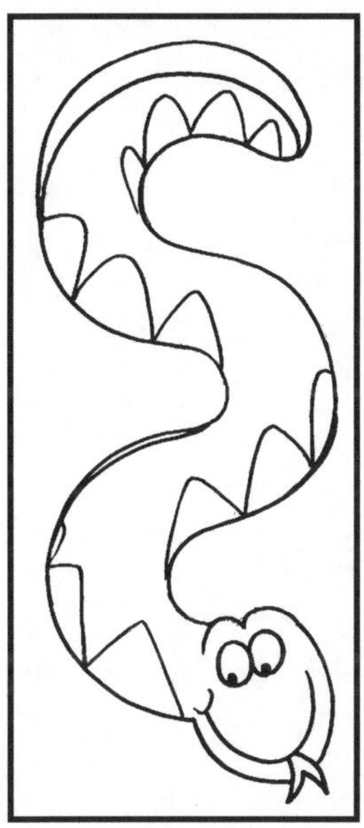

146 **Fly away maze**: C controls the toy airplane

147 **Time for lunch:** from top to bottom 5, 1 and 4 sausages are left

149 **I Spy unusual buildings:** from top right clockwise the buildings are AIRCRAFT HANGAR, MOSQUE, CINEMA,,APARTMENT, CATHEDRAL, CASTLE, and LIGHTHOUSE

Answers

Page

150 **Fast and slow**: of the four pairs, these are the fastest – RABBIT, AIRPLANE, TRAIN and TIGER

151 **Weather wordsearch**:

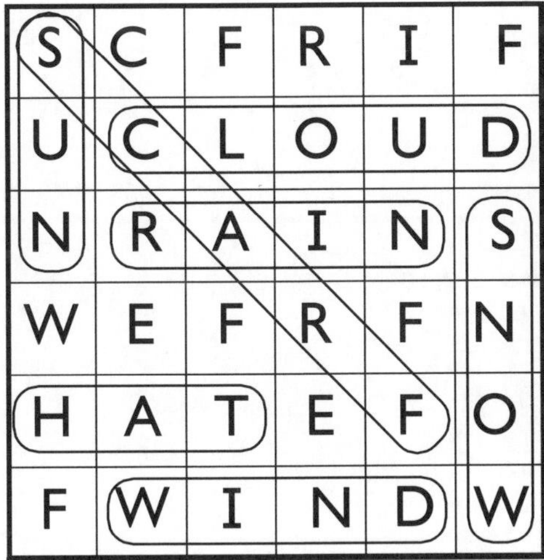

152 **Find the word:** the words are ANTELOPE, GIRAFFE, MONKEY, MOUSE, CROCODILE and ELEPHANT

153 **Dog's life:** DUSTY

Page

155 **Matching pairs**: the balloons match like this

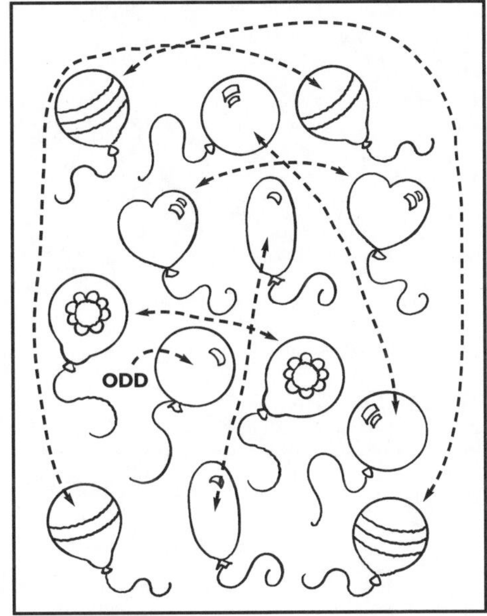

156 **Puzzle ice :** the flavor is VANILLA

157 **Connect the dots:** a group of lions is called a PRIDE

Answers

Page		Page	

158 Amazing: crocodiles are REPTILES

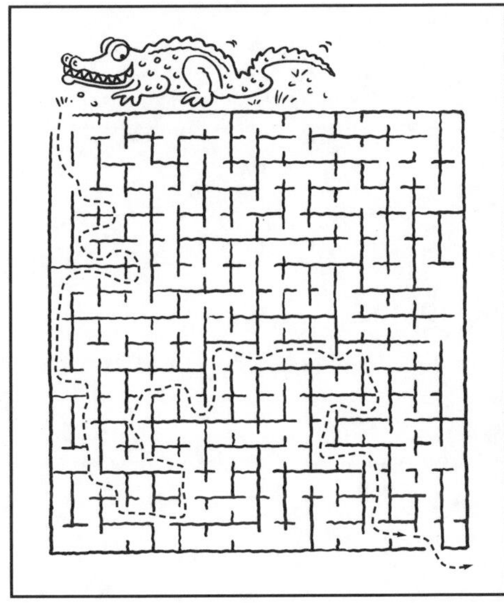

159 Star track:

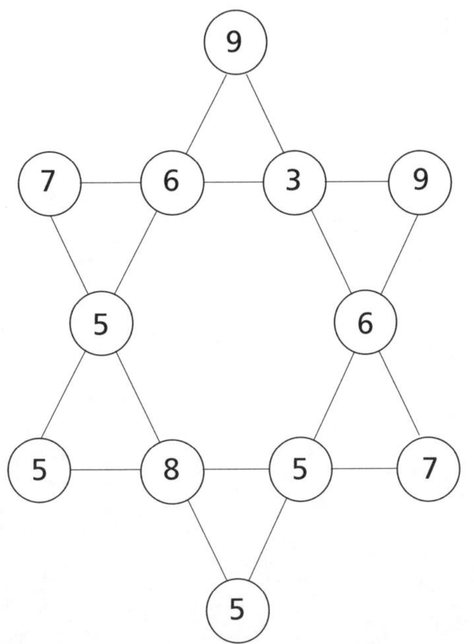

160 I Spy sea creatures: 4, the creatures are FISH, CRAB, STARFISH and SHELLFISH

162 Treasure hunt: 6, 8, 2, 12, 2, 4, 16, 18, 20 and 4

163 Find the city: the cities are NEW YORK, PARIS, LONDON, MOSCOW and BERLIN

164 Go on then: WHAT DID THE BOY SAY TO THE FROG? HOP IT

166 Words and pictures:

Answers

Page

167 **Fun quiz:** 1. PARIS, 2 ONION, 3 PETE SAMPRAS (he is a tennis player)

169 **Who is out there**? a MONKEY

170 **Too sweet for you:** 42, 38, 34 and 40 chocolates are left (from top left to bottom right)

172 **I Spy:** there are 11 PYRAMIDS

174 **Space search**:

A	V	C	B	K	S	P
S	P	E	N	O	S	L
P	L	A	N	E	T	U
M	A	R	S	U	N	T
O	S	T	A	R	S	O
O	K	H	W	S	S	J
N	S	A	T	U	R	N

Page

175 **Spot the word**: the word is LAUGH

176 **Aztec:** the message reads THE VOLCANO WILL ERUPT TONIGHT

178 **Matching pyramids**: they should be joined

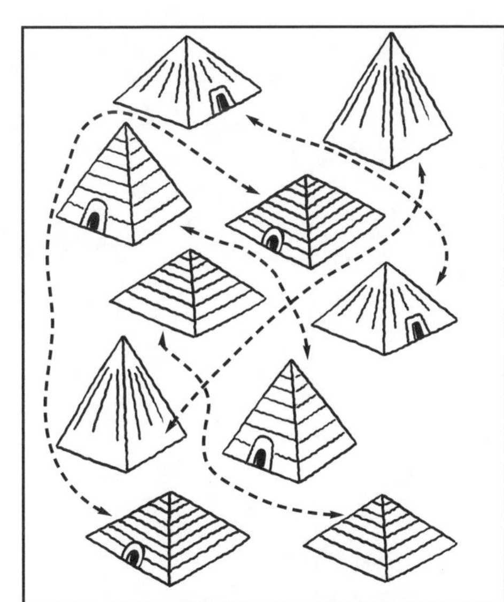

179 **Fun quiz:** 1 RED, 2 ORANGES, 3 GIRAFFE, 4 EDWARD (because it is a boy), 5 FRANC

Answers

Page

181 **Pirate's maze:**

182 **Spycatcher:** THE SPY WILL BE DRESSED AS A MILKMAN

183 **One track line:** the numbers are 1, 2, 3, 4, 5, 6, 7, 8, 9, 10, 11,12 and 13 the numbers add up to 91

185 **Spot the sun cream**: there are 9 TUBES of SUN CREAM

Page

186 **Half a zebra**: the related animal is the HORSE

187 **Spycatcher:** the spy is the UNCLE

188 **Lined up**: the six bird names are EAGLE, SWALLOW, ROBIN, JAY, NIGHTINGALE and BLACKBIRD

189 **Lost in Egypt:** the message says FOLLOW THE SUN UNTIL YOU SEE A TREE

191 **Matching pairs**: this is the odd one out

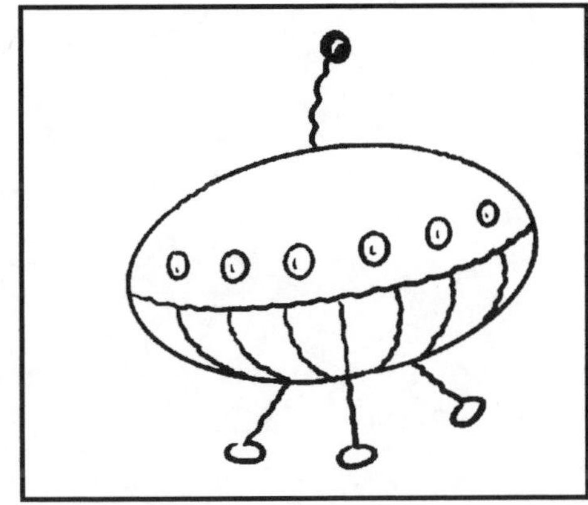

Answers

Page

192 **Lost in space rebus:** the greeting from space is HELLO THERE

193 **High Q**

194 **To the airport:**

Page

195 **Ready for tea:** they have eaten 8 sandwiches

196 **Spot the sea creatures**: the SEVEN different creatures are CRAB, FISH (various), PRAWN, SQUID, JELLYFISH, STARFISH and SHELLFISH

198 **Moon walker**: man first walked on the moon in 1969 (Neil Armstrong on July 21st)

199 **Detective wordsearch:** the words are HIDDEN, CLUE, SECRET, MESSAGE, DETECTIVE, NOTES, COVERT, CODE, SPY

200 **Puzzle fruits:** the fruit is an ORANGE

Answers

Page

201 **Message in a bottle:** the message says BLIND JACK HAS THE TREASURE MAP

203 **Tasty bites:** the seven foods are PIZZA, CAKE, COOKIE, COCONUT, BANANA, TOMATO, APPLE

205 **Crushing**

206 **On the Nile:** the right river is C

Page

207 **Anyone for tennis?** answers from top left to bottom right are 9, 3, 5, 7, 8 and 6

209 **I Spy odd things**: the six odd things on the beach are – PAN floating in the SEA, FIRE EXTINGUISHER, CHICKEN, SQUIRREL, SWIMMER in WINTER CLOTHES and a LIGHTHOUSE in the SEA (this should be on the cliff)

210 **Color fun**: Elephants are found in AFRICA and INDIA (and zoos of course!)

211 **Wordsearch:**

M	A	R	S	Z	U	L	A	R
A	J	U	P	I	T	E	R	R
R	X	Y	A	S	P	T	O	N
T	G	G	C	A	T	X	C	E
I	O	U	E	N	Y	O	K	T
A	V	N	O	O	M	Z	E	N
N	F	B	P	E	Z	A	T	S
Y	A	G	T	P	E	F	N	T

Answers

Page

212 **Word gaps:** the three letter words are – Group 1 ROT, Group 2 ART and Group 3 PET

214 **Word pairs:** the new phrases/words are: TEASPOON, FLAT FISH and MOUSE HOLE

215 **Fun quiz:** spy a is going to AUSTRALIA

216 **It's not nice:**

Page

217 **Aztec maze:**

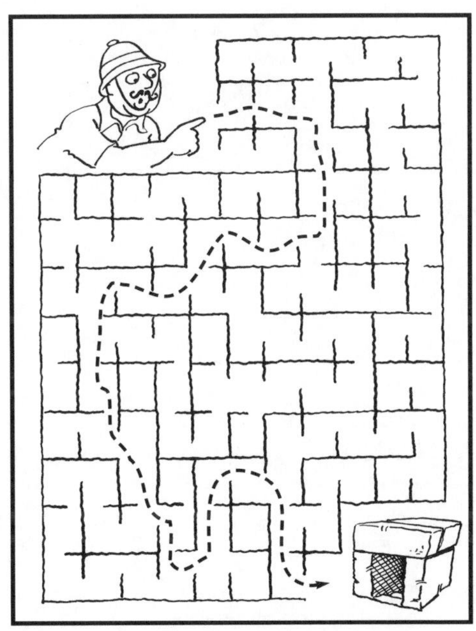

218 **More milk please:** THE DADDY COW does not give any milk; it is a BULL!

220 **I Spy ice** : there are FIVE complete ices in the picture

Answers

Page		Page	

221 **Spycatcher:** the names of the cities are Amos Cowlus = MOSCOW, Macai Robert = CAIRO, Agnew Yorkman = NEW YORK, Avalon Donald = LONDON, Mohammad Ridon = MADRID, Steve Nice = VENICE

223 **Lost words:** the flying object is a KITE

224 **Bird anagrams:** ROBIN, CROW, FINCH, WREN, JAY, WAGTAIL and THRUSH

226 **Word pairs:** the new words/phrases are: TABLECLOTH, APPLE PIE and MAILBOX

227 **Dotty cat**

228 **Escape maze:** 007 should take road E to make his way to the airport

229 **Sea letters:** there are 50 complete o's and 8 that are partly hidden

Answers

Page

232 Coded picture: the spy is operating a radio

233 Lost words: the hiding sea creature is a CRAB

234 Vacation signs: the countries are GREECE, USA, ENGLAND, ITALY, MEXICO and JAPAN

236 Pictures and letters: T is for TREE, B for BLOCK, M for MOON, D for DOLL, S for STAR, E for EGG

Page

237 Flying tonight?

238 Spy words anagram: BINOCULARS, PEN, TELESCOPE, TAPERECORDER, SUNGLASSES, GLOVES

240 Circle it: there are 18 complete circles (the man's eyes only count as one, because one of them is not a complete circle)

241 I Spy: the words include: APPLE, ACORN, ANIMAL, AIRPLANE, ANT and ANTENNA

Answers

Page

243 Suitcase wordsearch:

T	A	R	S	K	I	R	T
P	I	H	P	D	O	L	L
P	Y	J	A	M	A	S	S
R	R	M	D	A	G	U	H
L	D	R	E	S	S	N	O
D	I	T	R	E	N	H	R
B	U	C	K	E	T	A	T
G	T	S	H	I	R	T	S

244 Games and sports: the games are TENNIS, CRICKET, GOLF, SWIMMING and SAILING

246 Matching pairs:

Page

247 Police hideout: in a CASTLE

248 How many? there are FIVE different fruits ORANGES, PEARS, STRAWBERRIES, RASPBERRIES and APPLES

249 I Spy Ds: 7 things that begin with D are DUCK, DECKCHAIR, DRIVER, DAISY, DOOR, DISH (aerial) and DOG

250 Petsearch: RABBIT, FROG, DOG, CAT, GERBIL and HAMSTER

251 Anagrams: the words are: SPORTS, TENT, WATER, RIVERS, SUNSHINE and FUN

253 Matching pairs: PAN and MAN, SOCK and CLOCK, TAP and MAP, BED and HEAD

Answers

Page

254 **Spycatcher:** take the first word of each sentence to read SEE YOU IN THE TOY SHOP

255 **Connect the dots:** 007's holiday home is a YACHT

257 **Travel search:**

T	F	P	T	H	R	V	U	G	T
H	T	G	L	G	C	A	R	F	E
R	L	H	T	A	M	N	T	O	L
B	I	K	E	T	N	G	U	C	O
U	N	T	O	A	O	E	R	Z	R
H	E	L	I	C	O	P	T	E	R
H	R	F	Z	O	T	P	R	E	Y
T	O	R	N	A	D	B	U	S	N
I	B	H	M	C	I	Z	C	Z	E
Y	T	O	W	H	L	Q	K	R	R

258 **Broken words:** the countryside words are: CHURCHES, HEDGE, LANES, BIRDS, BADGER and STREAM

259 **Dotty detective:** the detective is SHERLOCK HOLMES

Page

260 **Spycatcher:** the spy's friend is MISS MONEYPENNY

262 **Wordsearch:**

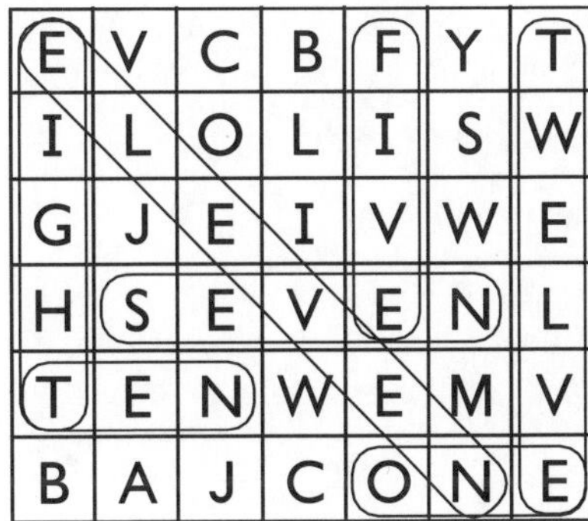